BOXING
On This Day

BOXING
On This Day
History, Facts & Figures
from Every Day of the Year

Nick Parkinson

BOXING
On This Day

History, Facts & Figures from Every Day of the Year

All statistics, facts and figures are correct as of 1st July 2015

© Nick Parkinson

Nick Parkinson has asserted his rights in accordance with the Copyright, Designsand Patents Act 1988 to be identified as the author of this work.

Published By:
Pitch Publishing (Brighton) Ltd
A2 Yeoman Gate
Yeoman Way
Durrington
BN13 3QZ

Email: info@pitchpublishing.co.uk
Web: www.pitchpublishing.co.uk

Published 2015

ISBN 9781785310522

Typesetting and origination by Pitch Publishing.
Printed in Malta by Melita Press

DEDICATION

For Caroline, George, Oliver and Teddy

ACKNOWLEDGEMENTS

Thanks firstly to Pitch Publishing for giving me the opportunity to write my first book, which I have thoroughly enjoyed working on. Thanks also to my wife Caroline and our three boys – George, Oliver and Teddy – for putting up with me when I start talking excitedly about boxing. Thanks also to my dad, Alan, for his proof-reading.

For research, I've used a lot of books, newspaper cuttings and video footage of fights (most of which can now be found online). There are too many names to include here but thanks to all my fellow journalists who have reported on boxing down the years, boxing historians and others involved in the media or boxing industries. Without their reports, statistics and accounts, this project would not have been possible. Thanks, in particular, to those at www.boxrec. com, an excellent source for boxing statistics and information.

Lastly, thanks to the boxers themselves who are featured in these pages.

INTRODUCTION

It is hard to think of a sport where history matters more than in boxing. The fight game is regularly looking back over its shoulder to mark anniversaries of big fights, remember glorious eras and to measure heroes of the fluorescent present against those of the sepia-toned past.

Boxing may have become a marginalised sport in recent years, but its epic encounters are known all over the world. Those that don't know the difference between a left hook and a fishing hook could still name boxing's big fights and its brightest stars.

People have forever been saying boxing was better in the past, but the sport is still capable of producing special moments and fighters to rank among the best in history. When Floyd Mayweather Jr and Manny Pacquiao finally met in May 2015, it was the biggest fight since at least the 1980s and the richest ever in pugilistic history. The long-anticipated world welterweight title fight captured a mainstream audience around the world, an occurrence that has been increasingly rare in recent decades.

In the UK, as in most countries, boxing has suffered from a diminished audience as it has been squeezed off regular showings on free-to-air television. Fight fans now have to seek out their sport as if on a treasure hunt, tracking down latest news on websites, social media and watching fights mostly on cable television channels. Although boxing can no longer be found regularly on UK terrestial television, it is still capable of capturing the public's imagination: Carl Froch's world super-middleweight title rematch with George Groves in May 2014 was British boxing's biggest fight since the Second World War.

In this book, I've tried to include a mixture of events from the recent era going back over a hundred years, featuring fights and incidents that were significant or memorable across the world. Apologies if some of your favourites are not included here as there were difficult choices for some days and I wanted to ensure there was some variety. I've attempted to include a broad spectrum of boxers and nationalities, from the heroic to the villainous and from the amusing to the sad.

I hope this book provides an entertaining journey back through boxing history enabling the reader to reminisce or perhaps learn something new about the sport, which still has plenty of fight left in it.

Nick Parkinson, June 2015

BOXING
On This Day

History, Facts & Figures
from Every Day of the Year

January

1st JANUARY 1923

Harry Greb was as wild in the ring as he lived out of it and in the year he won the world middleweight title, he met his match for fighting dirty. This was the second of three fights in four months with Bob Roper, who was knocked out of the ring in the fifth round. When Greb leant between the ropes offering a hand to his stricken opponent, Roper could not resist the opportunity to land two punches on his unsuspecting opponent. Roper – 20 pounds heavier – smacked Greb after the bell in the ninth and tenth rounds during a foul-filled scrap in which even the referee was hit twice before Greb was given the ten-round decision. "Prize fighting ain't the noblest of arts and I ain't its noblest artist," said Greb, AKA The Human Windmill.

2nd JANUARY 1957

Sugar Ray Robinson is widely regarded as the best ever boxer but at 35 he was past his prime when he met Gene Fullmer in a second defence of his world middleweight title at Madison Square Garden. Robinson had speed, silky skills, timing, bravery and power but by now he was slower and the reflexes were waning. He had even retired in 1952, only to make a comeback in 1955 and had soon regained the title. Fullmer, a 25-year-old Mormon from Utah, was fresher and the 15-round points decision was unanimous in his favour after he had floored Robinson in the seventh round. But Robinson was not finished. In a rematch the following May, Robinson won back the title for a fourth time after knocking out Fullmer with a single left hook.

3rd JANUARY 2007

Edwin Valero did not hang about in the ring. The Venezuelan blasted away his first 18 opponents inside the first round before being extended to two and then ten rounds. In the first defence of his WBA world super-featherweight title against Mexican Michael Lozada, he took just 72 seconds to register a 19th first round stoppage win. Valero seemed destined to become one of the biggest stars of his era after this fight but he never fulfilled his full potential as three years later, aged 28, he committed suicide in a police cell after stabbing his wife to death.

4th JANUARY 1940

World welterweight champion Henry Armstrong looked like he might finish Joe Ghnouly early after knocking him down three times in the opening round, but his fellow St Louis boxer got on his bike to avoid further punishment in the next few rounds. Armstrong caught up with Ghnouly early in the fifth round and finished him with three successive left hooks. Astonishingly, Armstrong defended his world title with a ninth round win over Pedro Montanez just 20 days later. Known as Homicide Hank, Armstrong held the featherweight, lightweight and welterweight world titles at the same time briefly in 1938.

5th JANUARY 1971

Sonny Liston's bloated dead body was the horrifying sight that greeted his wife Geraldine when she returned from holiday to their Las Vegas home. Her husband had been dead six days. Police attributed cause of death to a heroin overdose and a post mortem's verdict was lung congestion. Another theory is that Liston, who had a life-long fear of needles, was killed by an enforced heroin overdose administered by a Mob hitman. Liston won the world heavyweight title in 1962 but two years later was shown up by Cassius Clay's speed of mouth, hands and feet. Liston lasted 60 seconds in a rematch with Clay/Muhammad Ali after being stopped by a "phantom punch". There were suspicions both Clay/Ali fights were fixed by the Mob via Liston and the FBI investigated the first fight.

6th JANUARY 1928

Tommy Loughran looked doomed after he was given the second nine count in the first round of his world light-heavyweight title defence against Leo Lomski at Madison Square Garden. But Loughran, from Philadelphia, recovered to box his way to a 15 round decision for a second defence. Boxing on the undercard was Jim Braddock, who would lose to both Loughran and Lomski over the next two years before later re-emerging as a heavyweight known as Cinderella Man. Loughran stepped up to heavyweight after beating Braddock in 1929.

7th JANUARY 1995

Kevin Kelley suffered his first defeat and lost the WBC featherweight title after both eyes swelled over and his corner pulled him out of his third defence against Alejandro Gonzalez at the end of the tenth round. Kelley was put down in the sixth round but then floored Gonzalez in the eighth before both eyes closed over. Gonzalez, a 21-year-old from Guadalajara in Mexico, had pulled off a shock in Texas in only his second appearance on American soil. Gonzalez then made two successful defences.

8th JANUARY 1995

Carlos Monzon, a former world middleweight champion of seven years who was never knocked out, was killed when the car a friend was driving crashed. Monzon was 52 and was on his way back to prison after parole in his native Argentina. He spent the last five years of his life incarcerated after being sentenced to 11 years for the murder of his lover, Alicia Muniz, in 1988. Monzon, who retired in 1977, was convicted of killing Muniz, who fell from a second floor balcony at a party early on Valentine's Day 1988. Monzon's first wife had shot him and he had a record of assault and drunkenness, as well as possessing a gun, in what was never a quiet retirement.

9th JANUARY 1900

The first big fight of the 20th century saw American 'Terrible' Terry McGovern knock out Canadian George Dixon in eight rounds at New York's Broadway Club. McGovern, at 19, was ten years younger than the defending world featherweight champion and caught Dixon at the right time. But Dixon – known at the time as 'Little Chocolate' – dominated the early rounds and floored the challenger for the first occasion in his career in the fifth round. The older champ, who had been at the top a decade, then slowed and McGovern's energy and power saw him take control. Dixon went down eight times in the eighth and had to be rescued by his corner throwing in the sponge. McGovern's reign was shorter than Dixon's, lasting just two years, and both met premature deaths before they were 40. Dixon died of tuberculosis; McGovern, who was in and out of mental institutions after boxing and the death of his two daughters, died from pneumonia in 1918.

10th JANUARY 1976

Heavyweight contender Ken Norton claimed he took it easy on Pedro Lovell after stopping the Argentine in five rounds and staying on track for a third fight with Muhammad Ali later in the year. American Norton, aged 30, who was one of only two men at the time to have beaten Ali, forced a fifth round stoppage and then said: "I needed the work and didn't want to apply the pressure too soon because I hadn't boxed since August." Lovell is best remembered for playing the character Spider Rico in the first scene of *Rocky*, released later in 1976.

11th JANUARY 1997

Wayne McCullough not only lost a split decision in his WBC super-bantamweight title fight with Daniel Zaragoza, but also two wisdom teeth as well as suffering a broken jaw in the second round in Boston. The Belfast boxer, who had reigned as WBC bantamweight champion for two years before giving up the belt to face Mexican Zaragoza, finished strongly but it was not enough against Zaragoza, who at 39 was 13 years older than him. On the same night elsewhere in America, another Briton lost a world title fight but Londoner Kevin Lueshing gave IBF welterweight champion Felix Trinidad an early scare. Lueshing floored Puerto Rican Trinidad – unbeaten in 30 fights and rated one of the world's best pound-for-pound boxers – with a left hook in the second round. Trinidad only spent two seconds on the canvas and got up to halt Lueshing in the third round.

12th JANUARY 1959

Henry Cooper prevailed in a bloodbath with Brian London for the British and Commonwealth heavyweight titles at Earls Court, but defeat did the loser no harm. Cooper, who like London was cut around the eyes and bleeding from the nose, nullified the brawler in the second half of the fight as he jabbed his way to a points win. Our 'Enry might have got the decision to regain the titles and begin a 12-year reign as British champion, but it was London who got the opportunity to face world champion Floyd Patterson four months later. Cooper demanded $140,000 to face Patterson after beating London and Patterson opted to take on London instead. Cooper had to wait another seven years for his crack at the world title.

13th JANUARY 1921

It was the ringside presence of the Prince of Wales, later to become Edward VIII, which convinced Welshman Jimmy Wilde to commit fistic suicide against American Pete Herman. Wilde, the reigning world flyweight champion, was set to face the recently dethroned world bantamweight champion at the Royal Albert Hall. But Wilde then refused to fight after a row over the weigh-in time, which left his opponent with a big weight advantage. "The Prince of Wales came in to my dressing room and said if you don't fight there will be a riot here," said Wilde. Despite being at least two stones lighter, Wilde dominated early on but tired and was knocked out of the ring in the 17th round. Refusing to retire, referee Jack Smith lifted him up like a child and carried him back to his corner, saying: "I'm sorry Jimmy, but I have to pick you up because you don't know how to lie down." It was only Wilde's second loss in 150 recorded bouts.

14th JANUARY 1921

A day after Jimmy Wilde's stoppage across the Atlantic, those lucky enough to be at Madison Square Garden witnessed a thrilling first round as world lightweight champion Benny Leonard was floored once and his challenger Richie Mitchell three times in the opening session. Leonard was hurt badly and only just survived until the end of the first round, before forcing a sixth round stoppage. Leonard reigned as world champion for seven years.

15th JANUARY 2000

Brazilian Acelino Freitas dusted himself down from being sent sprawling by a left hook in the opening moments against Barry Jones – who had never knocked anyone out in an 18-fight career – to clinch an eighth round victory in defence of his WBO world super-featherweight title. Welshman Jones was dropped six times, twice later in an explosive first round, before his corner threw in the towel. "It's ironic really, the first time I put somebody down is the first time I get stopped," said Jones, who had been stripped of the same title after winning it in 1997 because he failed a brain scan. Jones never fought again.

16th JANUARY 1999

Mike Tyson was on one of his many comebacks and losing against Francois Botha when he planted a short right on the South African's jaw to bring an abrupt end in the fifth round of the heavyweight non-title bout. Botha crumpled to the canvas and stumbled as he tried to get up while Tyson wrapped his arms around his dizzy opponent to stop him falling through the ropes. That generous act of sportsmanship was in contrast to Tyson getting Botha into a lock and trying to break his arm at the end of the first round. This was former undisputed world champion Tyson's first fight since biting a chunk out of Evander Holyfield's ear in 1997.

17th JANUARY 1930

Jack 'Kid' Berg pulled off the best win of his career so far in the first of three encounters with American Tony Canzoneri at Madison Square Garden. The East Ender, who fought 74 times in America, outboxed ex-shoeshine boy Canzoneri for a split points decision over ten rounds that set up a shot at the world light-welterweight title the following month, which he won from Mushy Callahan back home in London.

17th JANUARY 2015

Deontay Wilder revived America's interest in the heavyweight division when he outboxed Bermane Stiverne for a unanimous decision in Las Vegas. The 6ft 7in Alabama resident, 29, earned the WBC title for extending his record to 33-0. It was the first time Wilder had been inconvenienced beyond four rounds as he became the first American to hold a portion of the world heavyweight title since 2006. "I just want to bring excitement back to the heavyweight division," said Wilder.

18th JANUARY 1962

Brazilian Eder Jofre unified the world bantamweight title with an impressive stoppage of Ulsterman Johnny Caldwell in front of 26,000 fans in Sao Paulo. After being knocked down in the fifth, the Belfast boxer – who was making a second defence of the European version of the world title – was behind on the scorecards when his manager jumped in to stop the fight in the tenth round. Jofre, one of the first vegetarian world champions, ruled as bantamweight champion from 1960 to 1964 and made a successful comeback in the early seventies. Caldwell lost a memorable British title fight with Freddie Gilroy later in the year, but was never the same.

19th JANUARY 1985

Colin Jones was outclassed when Don Curry visited to defend his WBA and IBF welterweight titles against the Welshman in Birmingham. American Curry won all three completed rounds before finishing the job 36 seconds into the fourth with Jones suffering a cut on the bridge of his nose from a razor-sharp jab which prompted the stoppage. Over 11,000 watched Jones's last fight and it was the first million pound gate in British boxing history.

20th JANUARY 2012

After winning gold medals at the 2000 and 2004 Olympic Games, Cuban Guillermo Rigondeaux defected from his communist homeland to live in Miami in 2009. Just nine fights into his professional career and he was recognised as WBA super-bantamweight champion and the best in his division after knocking out American Rico Ramos in the sixth round. Rigondeaux took control when he floored the champion with a straight right in the first round. Ramos was finished by a left to the body in the sixth. "Every time I let my hands go, I hurt him," Rigondeaux said. "I knew he wasn't getting up from that shot." It was performances like these that marked out Rigondeaux as someone to avoid in the super-bantamweight division.

21st JANUARY 2006

Manny Pacquiao got sweet revenge over Erik Morales with a tenth round stoppage as he further established himself as one of boxing's biggest global stars. The Filipino, who sold doughnuts on the streets during a childhood spent in abject poverty, was beaten on points by Morales in March 2005 but in the rematch Pacquiao was stronger. Morales was wobbled in the second and sixth rounds before being decked in the tenth and then stopped by the referee as Pac Man unloaded a furious assault. Morales was left on his hands and knees shaking his head. It was the first time Morales – a world champion at three weight divisions at the time – had been stopped and his third loss in four fights. They met again later in the year when Pacquiao would get the job done in three rounds.

22nd JANUARY 2002

Mike Tyson sunk his teeth into Lennox Lewis's thigh as a press conference to announce their world heavyweight title fight at New York's Millennium Hotel turned into a mass brawl. The fighters' teams clashed and as fists flew the WBC president Jose Sulaiman was knocked unconscious. "Somebody was biting my leg, so I pushed the head away, and it's Tyson biting my leg," said Lewis. Seven days later, the Nevada State Athletic Commission denied Tyson a boxing licence and so the fight took place in Memphis instead of Las Vegas. "I'm going to insist that he has a big lunch and a big dinner before he steps in there," said Lewis before their fight for his WBC and IBF world heavyweight titles.

23rd JANUARY 1968

Howard Winstone won a world title at the fourth attempt when he stopped Japan's Mitsunori Seki on a cut in the ninth round for the vacant WBC featherweight title in London. The artistic Welshman, who was also cut above an eye, had previously been beaten in three world title fights against Mexican Vicente Saldivar.

24th JANUARY 1930

A 17,692 crowd gathered at Madison Square Garden, eagerly anticipating the American debut of Italian giant Primo Carnera. Clayton 'Big Boy' Peterson was served up as an obliging victim and lasted 70 seconds, 25 of which were spent reclining in various positions on the canvas. Carnera received $17,904, although the rising star certainly did not see most of it as his sinister handlers got richer. The Ambling Alp, as he came to be known, was a mere tool of the boxing world that exploited his simple nature. Many of Carnera's fights were fixed by the Mob, including this one. Despite modest ability, he was built up with fixed fights and clever matching until he held the world title for a year from 1933. Once he was beyond protection as champion, his handlers let him fall and soon jettisoned him once he ceased being a money-maker. Carnera, who returned to

Italy in 1936 without much to show for his boxing career, was 6ft 6in and 270 pounds and was the biggest world heavyweight champion until 2006.

25th JANUARY 1894

James J Corbett had enjoyed his status as champion so much that newspaper previews believed his excessive drinking would land him in trouble against Charlie Mitchell. Corbett had not fought since he won the belt off John L Sullivan in 1892 to become the first world heavyweight champion under the Marquess of Queensberry Rules (three-minute rounds, a ten-second count for a knockout and the use of boxing gloves). But Corbett took control by flooring Mitchell late in the second round and in the third round Corbett knocked out the British challenger with a right flush on the chin.

26th JANUARY 2002

Vernon Forrest produced his finest performance to pull off the biggest upset of the year when he outpointed Sugar Shane Mosley for the WBC welterweight title. Mosley was boxing's No 1 star after taking the title from Oscar De La Hoya and did not have a blemish on his 38-fight record. Forrest, who was also unbeaten in 33 fights, stunned Mosley with a sharp combination that put him down twice in the second round and then used his jab to overcome Mosley's breathtaking hand speed. Forrest deservedly won a points decision over his fellow American – and it was the same story in a rematch six months later that earned Forrest $3.42million.

27th JANUARY 1913

'Peerless' Jim Driscoll was held to a draw with Birmingham's Owen Moran to retain his European version of the world featherweight title. The tired Welshman was put under siege late in the 20-round fight at the National Sporting Club in London that was the last big fight of Driscoll's impressive career. A clash between the pair had been six years in the making and there was added interest after Driscoll claimed it would be his last fight (but he fought three more times in 1919). Driscoll beat Abe Attell in New York four years previously and had been recognised as the world No 1 featherweight while Moran was a former world bantamweight champion. Driscoll went on to serve in the Army during the First World War and 12 years after facing Moran he died of pneumonia.

28th JANUARY 1995

Australia-based Russian Kostya Tszyu captured his first world title when he halted Puerto Rican Jake Rodriguez in the sixth round in Las Vegas. It was only Tszyu's 14th paid fight after turning professional and he grabbed the boxing world's attention with this crushing victory for the IBF light-welterweight belt. He knocked down Rodriguez in the first round and then four more times in the sixth before the fight was stopped. Tszyu remained at the top for the next ten years after staying in Australia following the 1991 world amateur championships in Sydney. On the same bill at the MGM Grand, the Ruelas brothers – WBC super-featherweight champion Gabriel and IBF lightweight king Rafael – defended their world titles.

29th JANUARY 2000

Julius Francis was so certain of not winning his fight with former world heavyweight champion Mike Tyson, that he sold the soles of his boots to a tabloid newspaper. The *Mirror* had their logo printed across the soles of Francis' boots which the world got to his see plenty of when the Londoner was deposited on the canvas in the second round on Tyson's European debut. The newspaper got good value for buying advertising space on Francis's shoes – Tyson knocked him down twice in the first round and three times in the second.

29th JANUARY 1973

Ken Buchanan had lost the world lightweight title to Roberto Duran the previous year but he was still too good for fellow Scot Jim Watt in their British lightweight title fight at St Andrew's Sporting Club in Glasgow. They are two legends of Scottish boxing and yet they met in front of just 600 people at a dinner show. In one of Buchanan's three outings in his homeland, he beat Watt 74¼-72½ on points. Watt would win the world title six years later, but a rematch with Buchanan never materialised. "I could not find one hard word to say against Jim Watt," said Buchanan. "It takes a man to do what he did tonight after 17 fights."

30th JANUARY 1982

Wilfred Benitez made his last world title defence aged 24 against Roberto Duran, who he beat by unanimous decision in Las Vegas. Benitez, the son of Puerto Rican immigrants who settled in New York, had become the youngest world champion in history in 1976 when he was 17 years, 5 months, and 23 days old. By the time he fought Duran for the WBC light-middleweight title, his best days were behind him and yet he still possessed enough ring-craft to tame the aggressive Panama idol. Benitez's purse of $1.4million was nearly three times as much as what Duran got but there was just one more (unsuccessful) defence and big fight in his career, against Thomas Hearns later that year. A decade later, Benitez was living off state support and suffering from pugilistic dementia.

31st JANUARY 1983

Caracas, the capital of Venezuela, hosted the first world title fight scheduled for 12 instead of 15 rounds when local hero Rafael Orono retained his WBC super-flyweight belt with a four round knockout of Panamanian challenger Pedro Romero. The governing body shaved three rounds off championship fights after recent deaths and injuries sustained in the ring.

BOXING
On This Day

History, Facts & Figures
from Every Day of the Year

February

1st FEBRUARY 1965

After being wiped out in a round twice by Sonny Liston in world heavyweight title fights, Floyd Patterson resurrected his career with a unanimous points win over Canadian George Chuvalo. In what was the richest non-title fight to date, there were gate receipts of $166,423 and $600,000 from theatre/cinema TV revenue. However, there were riots in Canada when there were technical problems in screening the fight. Patterson, the skilful former champion, seemed to be in trouble during the slugfest until flourishing in the ninth. "I can take it much better than you gentlemen give me credit for," Patterson told the media afterwards. Patterson's win earned him a shot at the new champion Muhammad Ali later that year.

2nd FEBRUARY 1982

Davey Moore was an eight-fight unbeaten novice when he travelled to Tokyo to challenge Tadashi Mihara – unbeaten in 15 fights – for the WBA world light-middleweight title. It was remarkable that the American had got his chance as No 1 challenger so soon, but he justified his opportunity by knocking out the Japanese hero in six rounds. After three knockout defences, Roberto Duran ended Moore's reign the following year and in 1988, aged 28, he was killed in a freak accident when he fell under his own car that was rolling down the driveway at his home.

3rd FEBRUARY 1993

Paul Hodkinson produced a career's best performance when he knocked out New York-based Puerto Rican Ricardo Cepeda at the start of the fourth round in a third defence of his WBC featherweight title in London. The Liverpool boxer, who was based in Belfast during his career, put himself on the brink of big pay-days and exciting TV deals by stopping Cepeda – but this would end up being his last win. Hodkinson agreed to fight American Kevin Kelley for $1million but first the Briton had to make a mandatory defence against Mexican Gregorio Vargas, who stopped him in April 1993. After another stoppage loss in 1994, all previous grand plans were forgotten and Hodkinson retired aged 28.

4th FEBRUARY 1952

Cuban Kid Gavilan was behind on the scorecards with two rounds remaining but had enough left to clinch a 15-round split decision over Bobby Dykes in Miami. Gavilan held on to his world welterweight crown in the first racially mixed bout to be held in Florida. Gavilan was an early star of the television era, boxing 22 times at Madison Square Garden and making 34 TV appearances. His best asset was the bolo punch, a long looping uppercut. Two decades before Muhammad Ali introduced the 'Ali Shuffle', the Cuban was doing his own dance routines in the ring and was later part of Ali's early training camps.

5th FEBRUARY 1943

Jake LaMotta handed the great Sugar Ray Robinson his first defeat when the Bronx Bull charged to a ten round unanimous points win at the Olympia Stadium, Detroit. Robinson, who had already beaten LaMotta in their first of six encounters in 1942, was unbeaten in 129 amateur and professional fights until his second meeting with LaMotta. The Bronx Bull, who outweighed Robinson by more than 16 pounds, softened up his rival with body shots in the first half of the fight. Robinson was sent sprawling through the ropes in the eighth and was up at the count of nine. The first professional defeat in 41 paid bouts hurt Robinson – it was in front of 18,930 in the city he grew up in – but he got revenge just three weeks later with a ten round decision back in Detroit.

6th FEBRUARY 1931

Watching Tommy Loughran box the ears of Max Baer among the 12,000 crowd at Madison Square Garden was James J Braddock. Loughran's ten round points win in a non-title heavyweight bout left an indelible impression on Braddock; he never forgot how Loughran used his educated left jab to make Baer look clumsy and avoid the Californian's big right hand. Baer would repair the damage done to his career and go on to rule as world heavyweight champion for one day less than a year. The man who relieved him of the title in 1935 was Braddock. "I seen Tommy Loughran lick him in the Garden," said Braddock. "I said to myself, if ever I fought Baer I'd do the same thing as Loughran done with him, the left hand and move."

7th FEBRUARY 1921

In the last of their 20 fights over six years, world welterweight champion Jack Britton beat Ted 'Kid' Lewis on a 15-round points decision in New York. American Britton's manager successfully objected to Lewis's use of a gumshield, because he reckoned it gave him an unfair advantage. The Londoner is believed to be the first boxer to use a protective mouthpiece in 1913. Britton won the series 4-3, with one draw and 12 no decisions. It was the last big fight East Ender Lewis had in America.

7th FEBRUARY 1997

In one of the saddest ends to a world heavyweight title fight, Oliver McCall disintegrated in an emotional and mental breakdown in the ring against Lennox Lewis. McCall's meltdown allowed London-born Lewis to regain his WBC belt, which he had lost when McCall knocked him out in 1994. McCall, an on-off drug addict who was in rehab the previous year for cocaine abuse, burst into tears at the end of the third round and began walking around the ring. The unstable American came out for the fourth in a trance, refusing to fight. When McCall turned his back in the fifth he was disqualified.

8th FEBRUARY 1924

World flyweight champion Pancho Villa, known as the Filipino Flash, beat Georgie Marks by a 15-round decision in New York – but the title was not on the line after the challenger weighed in four pounds over the limit. Villa, whose real name was Francisco Guilledo, had beaten Welshman Jimmy Wilde for the belt the previous year and comfortably dealt with the heavier Marks with his whirlwind style. This was Villa's last performance at Madison Square Garden in a brief reign; he died aged 23 the following year from blood poisoning after having a wisdom tooth extracted the day before his last fight against Jimmy McLarnin.

9th FEBRUARY 1974

After dominating the welterweight division for five years, Jose Napoles discovered he was just not big enough to conquer the middleweight scene when he failed to come out for the seventh round against Carlos Monzon in Paris. The Argentine, who had

SUGAR RAY ROBINSON HAS JAKE LAMOTTA IN TROUBLE IN 1951

a five-inch reach and six-pound weight advantages, retained his WBA-WBC world middleweight titles and would reign for another three years; the following year, Mexico-based Cuban Napoles lost his welterweight title.

10th FEBRUARY 1928

Tony Canzoneri won his first world title when he earned the featherweight belt for a 15-round split decision over Benny Bass, who broke his collarbone in the third round, in New York. Canzoneri went on to win world titles at lightweight and light-welterweight.

10th FEBRUARY 1992

Mike Tyson, 25, was convicted of raping Desiree Washington, an 18-year-old contestant in the Miss Black America beauty contest, in an Indianapolis hotel room. The former world heavyweight champion would serve half of a six-year sentence after being found guilty of one count of rape and two counts of deviate sexual conduct.

11th FEBRUARY 1990

No American venue would host Mike Tyson's world heavyweight title defence against James 'Buster' Douglas as it was deemed such a mismatch. It ended up in Tokyo and being arguably the biggest upset in boxing history. Douglas, a 42-1 no-hoper, took advantage of the champion's poor preparation to floor him for the first time in his career and then knock him out in the tenth round. Douglas was motivated by grief after the death of his mother 23 days before the fight while Tyson trained on a diet of women and late nights. Unlike those before him, Douglas was not intimidated by Tyson and after surviving a knockdown in the eighth produced a sharp combination to leave Tyson stretched out. Promoter Don King afterwards tried to get the result overturned as he claimed Douglas profited from a long count in the eighth.

12th FEBRUARY 1971

The most Ken Buchanan was shaken on his trip to Los Angeles to fight Ruben Navarro was by an earthquake in the days before their fight for the WBA and vacant WBC lightweight titles. The Scot had to contend with more trouble in the days before the fight than the

Mexican managed to give him in the ring. Navarro was only drafted in at 72 hours' notice to replace the injured Mando Ramos. There was then a change of hotel, emergency fillings in three teeth, a row over ensuring a British judge and a neutral referee and an attempt to dope the water bottle in his corner on the night of the fight. Buchanan started slowly, losing the first four rounds, but Navarro tired and Buchanan's jab earned him a convincing points decision.

13th FEBRUARY 1993

It was billed as 'Two Angry Men' and American rivals James Toney and Iran Barkley were certainly that ahead of their world super-middleweight title clash after a bitter war of words. But Toney, 24, kept his emotions in check in the ring as he opted to box rather than brawl as he expertly dismantled the champion, whose face was left disfigured by lumps. Toney lifted the IBF belt after the ringside doctor advised Barkley, 32, should be stopped after the ninth round since he could barely see out of either eye.

14th FEBRUARY 1951

Jake LaMotta often said, "I fought Sugar Ray Robinson so many times I got diabetes," and it was their last of six meetings that was the most painful for LaMotta. It is known as 'The St Valentine's Day Massacre', named after the 1929 shoot-out involving gangster Al Capone because of the bloody beating LaMotta took in the latter rounds. Robinson, who had been welterweight champion for four years from 1946, lifted the world middleweight title after stopping LaMotta on his feet in the 13th round at Chicago Stadium. Robinson elegantly dismantled the brawler with sharp jabs and damaging counter punches until LaMotta, who was subject of the hit film *Raging Bull* starring Robert De Niro, could barely stand. Robinson won their series 5-1.

15th FEBRUARY 1978

"I'm the latest, but he's the greatest," said new WBC-WBA world heavyweight champion Leon Spinks after dethroning Muhammad Ali on a split points decision in Las Vegas. Spinks, the 24-year-old who won light-heavyweight gold at the 1976 Olympics and had a comical gap-toothed grin, had only boxed seven times professionally when he upset the 8-1 odds. "I kept waiting for him to run out of gas but he never did," Ali said, who was making an 11th defence. Spinks, 24, was sharper, busier and finished the stronger. Ali, at 36, was left hanging on late in the fight and although he won a rematch later in the year, this was the beginning of the end for Ali, who lost three of his last four fights. It was the pinnacle of Neon Leon's career and by the time of the rematch he had been arrested four times for driving offences and drug possession.

16th FEBRUARY 1970

Joe Frazier began a three-year reign as undisputed world heavyweight champion after his pounding left hook overwhelmed Jimmy Ellis at Madison Square Garden. Muhammad Ali had been stripped of the title after he refused to be drafted into the US Army and an undisputed champion for the heavies was overdue with the vacant WBC belt and Ellis's WBA strap on the line. Smokin' Joe had a bobbing and weaving style, relentlessly stalking his opponents as he did Ellis, who was a sparring partner of Ali and had the same trainer, Angelo Dundee. It was Dundee who pulled Ellis out of the fight at the end of the fourth. "Gee, Angelo, I was OK, I was only put down once," said Ellis. Dundee replied: "You were put down twice, but you only remember once. That's why I stopped the fight."

17th FEBRUARY 1966

World heavyweight champion Muhammad Ali was told he was eligible to be drafted by the US Army for the Vietnam War after his draft status was reclassified from exempt, after failing an aptitude test, to 1-A. With war raging in Vietnam, the American government said standards had been lowered to bring in more soldiers. "For two years the government caused me international embarrassment, letting people think I was a nut," said Ali. "Now they make me 1-A without a test. Why did they let me be considered a nut for two years?" Ali would refuse the draft as a conscientious objector after claiming: "I ain't got nothing against them Viet Cong." The subsequent court cases meant Ali was out of the ring between March 1967 and October 1970.

18th FEBRUARY 2012

British boxing's reputation was left as tattered as an old boxing glove after David Haye and Dereck Chisora turned a humdrum post-fight press conference into a violent punch-up in Munich. Chisora had just been outpointed by WBC heavyweight champion Vitali Klitschko when he left the top table at the press conference to walk past journalists and confront Haye. The pair then rolled around the room with fists flying. Chisora accused Haye of bottling him and threatened to 'shoot' his fellow Londoner. Even the trainers were hurt, with Haye breaking the jaw of Chisora's trainer Don Charles and Haye's trainer Adam Booth left with a cut head.

19th FEBRUARY 2000

Mexicans Marco Antonio Barrera and Erik Morales were two of the best lower-weight fighters of their era and first collided in a super-bantamweight world title unification fight following weeks of bad-mouthing. The pair came from rival regions – Barrera from Mexico City, Morales from Tijuana – and were vying to replace Julio Cesar Chavez as Mexico's leading boxing hero. They refused to touch gloves before 12 rounds of non-stop aggression for the WBC and WBO titles in Las Vegas; neither were there any handshakes after Morales won a debatable split points decision. Barrera landed the best punches, especially in the fifth, and Morales even touched down in the final round. But the story did not end here and Barrera sucker-punched Morales at a press conference before their second fight, won controversially by Barrera. The trilogy ended with another Barrera points win in 2004.

20th FEBRUARY 1993

"He deserved to be punished," said Julio Cesar Chavez after stopping Greg Haugen in the fifth round in front of a record crowd of 132,247 at the Azteca Stadium in Mexico City. Mexican Chavez was unhappy at some of American Haugen's pre-fight comments and took retribution in the ring, flooring his challenger within seconds before returning him to the canvas in the fifth and then peppering him with punches to prompt the stoppage. Haugen unwisely claimed Chavez had built his 84-0 record up on "Tijuana taxi drivers". He needed a 25-man security team on fight night yet still had urine and beer thrown at him as he made his way to the ring. Chavez underlined his status as boxing's pound-for-pound No 1 with this WBC light-welterweight title defence. He grew up in an abandoned railway carriage but became Mexican royalty with the crowd for Haugen beating the 120,470 who watched Gene Tunney-Jack Dempsey in 1926.

21st FEBRUARY 1989

Dennis Andries began his second of three reigns as world champion when he knocked out Tony Willis in the fifth round to lift the vacant WBC light-heavyweight belt in Tucson. Guyana-born Londoner Andries, 33, had lost the title to Thomas Hearns two years previously and upset the odds against unbeaten American Willis with a big left hook.

22nd FEBRUARY 1910

Ad Wolgast recovered from a knockdown in the 22nd round to finally break the resistance of Battling Nelson in the 40th round and capture the world lightweight title in California. It was the highlight of Wolgast's career in which he was involved in too many ferocious fights. In 1927 Wolgast – known as the Michigan Wildcat – was committed to a sanitarium for many years because he had become punch drunk.

22nd FEBRUARY 1987

Lloyd Honeyghan cheekily bumped off Johnny Bumphus when he bolted from his corner at the start of the second round to floor the startled American, who had not finished rising from his stool, with a left hook. "The bell went ding and I went dong," Honeyghan said. Honeyghan was deducted a point for his fast start, but moments later the Londoner finished the job on a dazed Bumphus. It led to the introduction of the ten second warning to allow fighters and corners to prepare for the start of a round.

23rd FEBRUARY 1939

Eric Boon and Arthur Danahar put on a thrilling show for the cameras at the Harringay Arena. It was the first publicly screened bout in Britain with cinemas showing it live. It was also the first fight the BBC televised and viewers were not left disappointed as both visited the canvas before Boon, known as the Fen Tiger, triumphed in the 14th round in defence of his British lightweight title. Boon got £3,000 for his night's work.

24th FEBRUARY 1989

Roberto Duran earned a close 12-round decision over Iran Barkley to become a four-weight world champion aged 37 and 22 years after his professional debut. After defeats to Thomas Hearns and Marvin Hagler, Duran returned to form to earn a split points decision. Barkley, who won the WBC middleweight title off Hearns, was staggered in the first round by an overhand right. The American then struggled to find his corner after being floored in the 11th round. Barkley could hardly see out of a swollen left eye and was caught by two overhand rights in succession. It swung the fight Duran's way. "I am like a bottle of wine," Duran said. "The older I get, the better I get."

25th FEBRUARY 1995

Nigel Benn-Gerald McClellan was savagely thrilling but, more than anything, it was sickening as the loser suffered life-changing injuries. McClellan was widely tipped to win and silenced the home crowd when he knocked Londoner Benn through the ropes in the opening round. It is disputed how long Benn took to get back in the ring, but he survived the early storm. Benn had to drag himself off the canvas again in the eighth, after sinking to his knees following shots to the head and belly, before overwhelming the American in the tenth to defend his WBC super-middleweight title for the seventh time. McClellan suffered brain damage from injuries sustained in the fight, needing around the clock care thereafter. "I can't say it was my best fight because he came out in a wheelchair, blind and 80 per cent deaf," said Benn.

26th FEBRUARY 1968

Lionel Rose was only 19 when he became the first Aboriginal boxer to win a world title after he outpointed local hero Fighting Harada by scores of 71-72, 70-72 and 69-72 in Tokyo. Australian Rose was a replacement opponent and lost the WBC-WBA world bantamweight titles the following year.

26th FEBRUARY 1926

Tiger Flowers pulled off an upset when he tamed the rough brawler Harry Greb over 15 rounds, earning the points decision and the world middleweight title at Madison Square Garden. Flowers, from Georgia, became the first black boxer since heavyweight Jack Johnson to hold a world title. In the 11 years since the end of Johnson's reign, black fighters had been blocked from fighting for world titles. Flowers was such a religious man that he recited passages from Psalm 144 before every fight and even brought the Bible into the ring before facing Greb, who enjoyed a hedonistic lifestyle. Flowers beat Greb in a rematch later in the year but died aged 34 in 1927 following an operation to remove scar tissue from around his eyes. Greb also died following surgery on a nose injury in 1926.

27th FEBRUARY 1902

World bantamweight champion Harry Forbes was successful on this day two years in succession, winning points decisions over Tommy Feltzj in 1902 and then Andrew Tokell a year later. Irish-American Forbes's reign was ended later in 1903 when he was knocked out by Frankie Neil.

28th FEBRUARY 1949

Ezzard Charles's unanimous 15-round split decision over Joey Maxim earned him a crack at a version (NBA) of the world heavyweight title and a year later he would face undisputed champion Joe Louis. Charles was Maxim's nemesis: this was one of five victories for Charles over Maxim, whose real name was Giuseppe Berardinelli. But Maxim, who was renamed after the Maxim machine gun because of his quick jabs, travelled to London the following year to beat Freddie Mills for the world light-heavyweight crown.

28th FEBRUARY 2009

Juan Manuel Marquez silenced Juan Diaz's home crowd in Texas with a ninth round stoppage as he continued his remarkable run of winning world titles at different divisions. Marquez, who would win world title belts in four divisions, captured the vacant WBO and WBA light-welterweight belts for dismantling Diaz in the ninth round. Diaz, cut in round eight, was leading on two of the judges' scorecards when a sharp combination dropped him in the ninth. He bravely got up but Mexican Marquez followed up with a right uppercut to finish.

29th FEBRUARY 1912

A month after his 18th birthday, glamorous Georges Carpentier won the European middleweight title when he knocked out Londoner Jim Sullivan in the second round in Monte Carlo. The Frenchman had previously campaigned at welterweight and this win boosted his popular image around Europe. Despite being smeared in blood by the end, Carpentier was mobbed by women who accounted for half the crowd at the Stand de la Condamine. Two years later, Carpentier's career was put on hold until 1919 while he served as a low-flying observation pilot in the French air force during the First World War, which earned him two of the highest French military honours. After having his first paid bout aged 13, Carpentier – known as The Orchid Man – boxed in every division from flyweight to heavyweight, winning the world light-heavyweight title in 1920, and France has not had a boxing hero of his like since.

BOXING
On This Day
History, Facts & Figures
from Every Day of the Year

March

1st MARCH 2003

Roy Jones Jr became the first former world middleweight champion to win a world heavyweight title since Bob Fitzsimmons in 1897 when he outclassed John Ruiz for the WBA belt. Jones, 34, broke Ruiz's nose with a right in the fourth as he cruised to his 48th win in 49 fights. Despite being outweighed by nearly 30 pounds, the American's dazzling hand speed earned a unanimous decision. He was the lightest boxer to challenge for a world heavyweight title since Floyd Patterson took on Archie Moore in 1956. Jones's legacy would be tarnished, however, the following year when he stepped back down to light-heavyweight and was knocked out by Antonio Tarver and Glen Johnson.

2nd MARCH 1996

Thulani 'Sugar Boy' Malinga was 40 and not expected to bother WBC world super-middleweight champion Nigel Benn too much. "I was complacent, I thought it was going to be an easy night," said Benn, whose right eye closed early in the fight en route to a split points defeat in Newcastle. South African Malinga, who had lost to Benn four years previously, got up from a right hand in the fifth. Londoner Benn announced his retirement in the ring afterwards before then proposing to his girlfriend Caroline. But Benn would fight twice more before the end of the year, while Malinga would lose the title in a first defence before winning it back in 1997.

3rd MARCH 1990

Lloyd Honeyghan was left so traumatised by his third round evisceration at the hands of Mark Breland that he briefly considered leaving the UK. The Jamaica-born boxer, who had lived in London since childhood, was floored six times in three humiliating rounds against WBA welterweight champion Breland. Honeyghan was finally stopped after being dropped three times in the third, with the Wembley crowd chanting 'What a load of rubbish'. Honeyghan was so hurt he sold his luxury apartment for a bargain and got ready to leave England. "I was so mad, I just wanted to go," he said. Honeyghan, undisputed champion from 1986 to 1987, had a change of heart but his career never recovered. For the tall and elegant Breland, it was his seventh successive knockout but in his next fight he lost the belt to Aaron Davis.

4th MARCH 2006

WBO super-middleweight champion Joe Calzaghe captured Jeff Lacy's IBF belt in a surprisingly one-side world title unification clash that many tipped the American to win in Manchester. Calzaghe floored Lacy in the last round before getting a unanimous decision, but the Welshman nearly pulled out prior to the fight due to a hand injury. "Lacy was my proudest fight because I was written off beforehand and I completely did a number on him," said Calzaghe, who retired undefeated after nearly 11 years as world champion. "Going into the fight with the injury I had, with all the negative press, I had a lot to prove and it felt great."

5th MARCH 1948

1948 – Gus Lesnevich needed only 118 seconds to knock out Billy Fox and retain his world light-heavyweight title at Madison Square Garden. Six straight rights floored Fox who staggered to his feet only to be flattened again and counted out for the second time in his career. Lesnevich, who served with the US Coast Guard during the Second World War, had ended Fox's impressive unbeaten record the previous year after he had stopped all 36 opponents. It was the American's last defence before losing to Britain's Freddie Mills.

6th MARCH 1964

A legend was born when Cassius Clay, the new world heavyweight champion, officially changed his name to Muhammad Ali. On February 26, a day after he had shocked the world by forcing Sonny Liston to retire on his stool at the end of the sixth round, Clay announced he had changed his name to Cassius X and joined the Nation of Islam. After a row between the black Muslim leaders Malcolm X and Elijah Muhammad, Clay sided with Muhammad who on March 6 instead gave him the name that would become the most famous on earth. "Cassius Clay is a slave name," said the champ. "I didn't choose it and I don't want it. I am Muhammad Ali, a free name – it means beloved of God, and I insist people use it when people speak to me and of me." Initially, many people still called him Clay, including opponents, much to Ali's chagrin.

7th MARCH 1987

Thomas 'The Hitman' Hearns successfully stepped up to light-heavyweight when he dethroned WBC champion Dennis Andries in his home city of Detroit. The Guyana-born Londoner was halted in the tenth round of a second defence after being outclassed by Hearns's speed and array of punches. Andries was floored four times in the sixth round before two more knockdowns towards the end. It was a masterful performance from Hearns, who less than a year earlier was light-middleweight champion. After losing to Hearns, Andries decided to join his conqueror's Kronk gym and hire his trainer Emanuel Steward. Under Steward, Andries would regain the title.

8th MARCH 1971

"You know, you're in here with the God tonight," said Muhammad Ali. "If you are God, you're in the wrong place tonight," replied Joe Frazier before their first of three epic encounters. It was called the 'Fight of the Century' and it was such a big event that crooner Frank Sinatra had to get accredited as a ringside photographer to be there. Frazier went into the fight raging about Ali calling him an "Uncle Tom". "He thought that would weaken me when it came time to face him in that ring," said Frazier. "Well, he was wrong." Ali's hand-speed won him the early rounds but he then slowed in the middle rounds. By the 11th round Smokin' Joe began to edge ahead in his WBA-WBC world heavyweight title second defence. Frazier kept perpetually bobbing forward and floored Ali with a thudding left hook to the jaw in the 15th and last round before triumphing unanimously on points (9-6, 11-4 and 8-6) at Madison Square Garden. It was Ali's first loss in front of an estimated 300million television viewers. Frazier spent weeks recovering in hospital. Ali, silenced at last, also went to hospital with a badly swollen jaw. During the excitement, one of the 20,455 spectators died of a heart attack.

9th MARCH 1912

Former world featherweight champion Abe Attell took a beating in a 20-round war with 'Harlem' Tommy Murphy, who weighed at least ten pounds more than him. Attell did not help himself though after going on an all-night gambling spree the night before the fight in California. Attell, from San Francisco, was in decline having lost the title a month previously.

JOE FRAZIER WALKS TO A NEUTRAL CORNER AFTER KNOCKING DOWN MUHAMMAD ALI IN 1971

10th MARCH 1986

John Mugabi extended 'Marvelous' Marvin Hagler to 11 rounds in a brave bid for the undisputed world middleweight title in Las Vegas. Uganda-born Mugabi, who won a silver medal for his country at the 1980 Olympics before basing himself in London as a professional, had won all 26 fights by KO by the time he faced Hagler. Mugabi survived a battering in the sixth and the pair went toe-to-toe before the champion caught Mugabi – known as 'The Beast' – with two big right hands. "I promised you I'd feast on the beast," said Hagler. "And I came to dinner." It would be the last victory of Hagler's career.

11th MARCH 1995

A head-butt in the second round from Herbie Hide awoke Riddick Bowe, who proceeded to floor his British opponent seven times in a sixth round victory. "If you head-butt me, I'm not going to shake your hand," said Bowe. "I'm going to beat the hell out of you the first chance I get." Hide got $3.2million for being bullied in Las Vegas and Bowe $1million, as well as the WBO heavyweight title which was lightly regarded at the time. Bowe, 27, had been undisputed champion three years previously and lost the WBA and IBF titles in 1993. This win, he hoped, would catapult him back into the big league.

12th MARCH 2011

Miguel Cotto silenced loudmouth Ricardo Mayorga with a 12th round stoppage. The Puerto Rican floored Mayorga with a left hook after a vicious exchange of blows. When the Nicaraguan got to his feet he went in retreat before shaking his head and asking the referee to stop it. Mayorga, who injured his left hand just before going down, was losing the fight with all three judges having WBA light-middleweight champion Cotto five rounds ahead. It was the last big fight of former champion Mayorga's career.

13th MARCH 1999

Lennox Lewis was victim of a New York mugging when judges returned a draw verdict following his world heavyweight title unification clash with American Evander Holyfield. Experts and fans around the world slammed the controversial decision after London-born Lewis, who brought the WBC title into the contest, seemed to clearly dominate WBA-IBF champion Holyfield at Madison Square Garden. Lewis landed 348 punches to Holyfield's 130. One judge, Eugene Williams, even gave the contest to Holyfield by two rounds while British judge Larry O'Connell scored it a draw. The other judge gave it to Lewis 116-113. It led to a rematch eight months later when Lewis punched his way to justice to become Britain's first undisputed world heavyweight champion since Bob Fitzsimmons 102 years earlier.

14th MARCH 1980

Jim Watt was in his prime but he had an early fright when Northern Irish challenger Charlie Nash put him down in the first round at the Kelvin Hall. Nash made a confident start, dumping Watt on his backside with a short right to the chin. But seconds later, Nash was bleeding from a cut above the left eye. Glaswegian Watt went on to floor fellow southpaw Nash three times in the fourth before it was stopped. Nash suddenly fell to pieces in the fourth round after being nailed by a left hand and was finished by the same punch. It was Watt's second defence of his WBC lightweight title and was the first time two British boxers had fought for a world title since 1949.

15th MARCH 1983

Charlie Magri completed a remarkable turnaround in fortunes when he won the WBC world flyweight title from Eleoncio Mercedes, who was stopped on a cut in the seventh round. The East Ender had suffered two stoppage defeats in the previous two years and Mercedes, from the Dominican Republic, was expected to retain his title. Mercedes was cut above his left eye by an accidental head-butt in the sixth round and in the seventh was rocked by a right hand before it was stopped due to the wound. "Nine months ago his career was in pieces and now he's world champion," said Magri's manager Terry Lawless.

16th MARCH 1996

Frank Bruno looked a beaten man on his way to the ring to face Mike Tyson in Las Vegas. The Londoner knew all about Tyson's frightening power: the American had stopped him in five rounds in

1989. Since then Tyson had served three years in jail for rape. Bruno, who was making the first defence of his WBC world heavyweight title, seemed paralyzed by fear and was predictably clubbed into a third round stoppage. Bruno went into the fight with a detached retina in his right eye. "I had to retire win or lose because I couldn't have gone on with my eye in that state," Bruno said.

17th MARCH 1897

Bob Fitzsimmons introduced the world to the debilitating solar plexus shot when he stopped James J Corbett in the 14th round for the world heavyweight title. Fitzsimmons, a former world middleweight champion who was born in Cornwall and moved to New Zealand aged 11, got off the canvas in the sixth round and, despite weighing 16 pounds less, went on to stop the American for boxing's most treasured possession in gold-digging Carson City. With his wife Rose screeching "Hit him in the slats Bob", the challenger dug a left fist into the solar plexus that dropped Corbett. Corbett tried to get up, clasping at the ropes, but fell on his face and was counted out.

17th MARCH 1990

Mexican Julio Cesar Chavez knew he had to stop Meldrick Taylor to preserve his unbeaten record and win their world light-welterweight title unification fight – and he did so with two seconds to spare. Taylor, the American Olympic hero of 1984 and IBF champion, was winning by a comfortable margin. But WBC king Chavez launched a furious assault in the last round and a couple of right-handers floored Taylor. When Taylor got up, referee Richard Steele waved the fight off with two seconds remaining.

18th MARCH 1995

After 14 defences of his WBO super-middleweight title, Chris Eubank was left spooked and beaten by Steve Collins. Eubank was rattled by Collins's claim he had been hypnotised into thinking he was invincible and suffered his first defeat of his ten-year career. Both touched down but it was Collins who got the unanimous decision and afterwards the Irishman admitted his hypnosis claim was a bluff.

JULIO CESAR CHAVEZ (RIGHT) LANDS A RIGHT ON MELDRICK TAYLOR IN 1990

19th MARCH 1943

Willie Pep was beaten for the first time in 63 fights by former world lightweight champion Sammy Angott. The previous year Pep had won a version of the world featherweight title aged 20 and fortunately for him it was not on the line when he was outpointed over ten rounds by Angott. It was one of just 11 defeats in 241 professional fights for Pep, who was world featherweight champion on and off for the rest of the decade. Ten days after losing to Angott, Pep got back to winning ways and went 73 bouts undefeated over the next five years. Pep was a masterful defensive boxer with sharp reflexes and known as Will o' the Wisp for his elusiveness. Pep served in the US Navy in 1943 and also in the US Army in 1945 during the Second World War.

20th MARCH 1976

East Ender John H Stracey made his only WBC world welterweight title defence against American Hedgemon Lewis at the old Wembley Arena. Stracey, who won the belt with a shock stoppage of Jose Napoles in Mexico, shook Lewis with a body shot in the sixth and had him rocking again in the ninth before Lewis succumbed in the 11th. Lewis never fought again after his third unsuccessful world title shot while Stracey would win just one of his next – and last – three fights.

21st MARCH 1997

For the first 15 years and 50 fights of his career there was only one blemish on Roy Jones Jr's professional record. It came when he was disqualified while hitting Montel Griffin with two punches while his fellow American was down on his knees in round nine. Little-known Griffin won Jones's WBC light-heavyweight title while lying on the canvas. "I wasn't sure he was down," said Jones. He was ahead on two judges' scorecards and behind on another at the time of the stoppage. It was the first fight Jones had lost since the gold medal bout at the 1988 Olympics, when he was controversially beaten on points by South Korea's Park Si Hun. Despite this loss in his 34th fight, Jones went on to be the most dominant fighter in the 1990s and was named 'Fighter of the Decade' by the boxing press.

22nd MARCH 1983

Michael Spinks was still in mourning when he outpointed Dwight Muhammad Qawi in a world light-heavyweight title unification clash. Spinks cried in the dressing before the fight over the death of his long-term girlfriend Sandra Massey in a car crash two months previously. He then went out to jab his way to a unanimous decision, rising from a controversial knockdown in the eighth round caused by Qawi stepping on his foot. Spinks survived a later rally from Qawi and celebrated in the ring with his two-year-old daughter. The fight nearly never happened after Qawi, who had recently changed his name from Braxton, was diagnosed with pneumonia a week before. Qawi accused Spinks of running after being frustrated by his fellow American's jab. Both went on to win world titles, at heavyweight (Spinks) and cruiserweight (Qawi).

23rd MARCH 1948

Rinty Monaghan became the first boxer from Belfast to win a world title with a seventh round victory over Scotsman Jackie Paterson which crowned him undisputed flyweight champion at the King's Hall. Monaghan floored Paterson with a right to the jaw in the second round and then again with a right to the body in the seventh. Paterson got up but moments later he was left crumpled in a heap in the corner. After stopping Glaswegian Paterson, Monaghan – known as Rin Tin Tin – led the crowd with a rendition of 'When Irish Eyes Are Smiling' from the ring.

24th MARCH 1962

In sickening scenes broadcast on national television live across America, Emile Griffith battered Benny 'Kid' Paret into a coma in the 12th round for the world welterweight title. Ten days later, Paret died from brain injuries. The two American immigrants had developed a fierce rivalry over two previous fights. "There was bad blood between us at the weigh-in. He called me maricon [in Spanish], which means faggot in English," said Griffith, who never publicly admitted his homosexuality until it was confirmed after his death in 2013. Paret dropped Griffith in the sixth, but then faded and found himself pinned against the ropes in the 12th. Griffith landed 17 clean and unanswered punches, including a succession of right uppercuts. Paret became limp and unconscious as he lay held up by the ropes while referee Ruby Goldstein crucially did not step in.

25th MARCH 1958

He had already retired and had been written off after defeats in two world title fights in the previous year, but Sugar Ray Robinson showed just why he is regarded as the best ever when he won the world middleweight title for an incredible fifth time with a 15-round split points decision over Carmen Basilio at Chicago Stadium. His real name was Walker Smith and he had the 'Sugar' added to his name because he boxed "as sweet as sugar". But at 36, Robinson was not flawless. Robinson, who lost the belt on a split decision to Basilio the previous September, shut Basilio's left eye in the sixth round with a slashing right hand on what was his last glorious night of an astonishing career. Robinson had lost the title to Basilio and Gene Fullmer, also in 1957, but in the rematches he showed his greatness – despite his decline – and ability to overcome any opponent. He lost the title to Paul Pender in 1960 but carried on boxing as an imitation of his former self until 1965.

26th MARCH 1974

Ken Norton had broken Muhammad Ali's jaw the previous year on the way to a shock win but he did not last two rounds when he challenged George Foreman for the world heavyweight title in Caracas, Venezuela. Foreman floored Norton three times in the second. Promoter Don King was so confident of Foreman's victory that he had already signed a deal for him to defend his titles against Ali next in a fight that would be known as 'The Rumble in the Jungle'. Both fighters were delayed in leaving Venezuela after the government insisted they paid taxes on their ring earnings.

27th MARCH 1925

An in-form Gene Tunney earned a comfortable ten round decision over world middleweight champion Harry Greb, who weighed 13 pounds lighter. "That's the last time I'll fight this guy," Greb said after the pair's fifth and final fight. "He's getting too big and too strong for me to handle. I could lick him at one time but not anymore. Tunney is really getting good." Greb finished their series a 3-1 winner, with one draw. A year after this meeting, Tunney was world heavyweight champion and Greb was dead.

28th MARCH 1998

Herol 'Bomber' Graham was left to forever be known as a nearly man when he was stopped in the tenth round by Charles Brewer for the IBF super-middleweight title in Atlantic City. Graham was the first major star to emerge from the Wincobank Gym in Sheffield under the watchful eye of maverick Irish trainer Brendan Ingle. In the last of three world title challenges, 37-year-old Graham dropped Brewer twice in the third round but the American – who was ten years younger – survived to force a tenth round stoppage. Shortly after, an eye injury led to Graham's retirement. Brewer, from Philadelphia, would have one more defence before losing the belt to Sven Ottke later in the year.

29th MARCH 1980

John Conteh was stopped for the first time in his career after a rematch with Matthew Saad Muhammad went horribly wrong for him in Atlantic City. After losing unanimously on points, Conteh had earned a return fight with Saad Muhammad for the WBC world light-heavyweight title after it was ruled the American's corner had used a banned substance to stem the flow of blood on a cut during their first fight. The American turned on the power in round four and Liverpool's former champion was put on the canvas five times before it was stopped. "He hit like a heavyweight and is the best man I fought," said Conteh, who had one more fight before retiring and whose private life was making headlines for the wrong reasons.

30th MARCH 1965

Willie Pastrano never fought again after failing to answer the bell for the tenth round against Jose Torres at Madison Square Garden. Pastrano was defending his world light-heavyweight title and was decked for the first time in his career by a shot to the kidney in the sixth round. Pastrano was bleeding from the first round and when he was asked by a ringside doctor during the fight if he knew where he was, Pastrano said: "You're damn right I do. I'm in Madison Square Garden getting the shit kicked out of me." In retirement, Pastrano won another battle with heroin addiction later in the sixties.

31st MARCH 1973

Ken Norton broke Muhammad Ali's jaw as he became the second man to beat The Greatest. The 12-round points decision was split but so too was Ali's jaw and after the NABF heavyweight title fight he said: "Imagine you have your jaw broken and have to fight ten more rounds." The result (7-5, 5-4 for Norton; 6-5 to Ali) was a shock since ex-Marine Norton was relatively unknown at the time and entered the fight a 5-1 underdog. But Ali avenged the loss with his own split decision win later that year in his pursuit of another world title shot. The Americans would meet once more in 1976 when Ali won more comfortably with the WBA and WBC world titles on the line.

31st MARCH 1980

Dave 'Boy' Green was the unfortunate recipient of what Sugar Ray Leonard describes as the best punch he ever threw. The left hook, delivered at the end of a blistering four-punch combination, flattened the British challenger in the fourth round. WBC world welterweight champion Leonard's celebrations quickly turned to concern for his stricken opponent. He said: "I hit the guy with a dynamite left hook and he was laid out. I really was scared for him." Green was left on his back for a few minutes before being scraped off the canvas by his corner.

BOXING
On This Day
History, Facts & Figures
from Every Day of the Year

April

1st APRIL 2000

Despite a comfortable points lead over American challenger Chris Byrd, Vitali Klitschko quit on his stool at the end of the ninth round due to a shoulder injury, a torn rotator cuff. It was the Ukrainian's first professional defeat and cost him a money-spinning US TV deal as well as his WBO version of the world heavyweight title. Critics also questioned Klitschko's heart after opting not to go through the pain barrier and there were doubts he would ever return to the top level. Byrd took the fight at only ten days' notice and lost the WBO belt in a first defence to Vitali's younger brother Wladimir. Vitali's shoulder mended and so did his career when he won back a world title belt four years later. After retiring through injury, Vitali then resumed his reign as WBC champion from 2008 until 2013.

2nd APRIL 1943

After winning world titles in three weight divisions, Henry Armstrong was on his way out and would be retired within two years when he met Beau Jack. Armstrong had been Jack's hero but by the time they met the former champion's failing eyesight nearly stopped the fight from happening. Jack earned a unanimous decision over ten rounds in one of his early performances at Madison Square Garden, one of 21 times he fought at the iconic venue. A month after beating Armstrong in front of 18,000, Jack lost his New York version of the world lightweight title on points to Bob Montgomery but won it back in a rematch six months later.

2nd APRIL 1971

Rubén Olivares quickly got up from a sixth round knockdown to win back the WBC-WBA world bantamweight titles in a third meeting with Chucho Castillo. Olivares was up at the count of three and quickly regained his composure at the Forum in California. After being stopped on a cut the previous year, Olivares well deserved revenge and got a unanimous decision over his Mexican rival to win the trilogy 2-1.

3rd APRIL 1976

Rigoberto Riasco became the first world super-bantamweight champion in history when he knocked out Wainunge Wakayama in ten rounds in Panama for the WBC's vacant title. The WBA had their first world super-bantamweight fight the following year by which time Riasco had lost his WBC belt.

4th APRIL 2009

It was a new division but same old story as Edwin Valero stopped Antonio Pitalua in the second round, his 25th KO victim from as many fights to win the WBC lightweight title. Nothing it seemed could stop the destructive Venezuelan but a year later he would be dead. Valero was found hanging in a police cell after admitting to the murder of his wife and following recent treatment for alcohol and drug dependency.

5th APRIL 1915

Jess Willard prevailed in the longest world heavyweight title fight in history (one hour and 44 minutes) when he knocked out the first black world heavyweight champion Jack Johnson in the 26th round. Johnson later claimed he took a dive in Havana, Cuba in return for immunity from the law on previous spurious – and racist – charges against him. Johnson, 37, was on top until he began to tire and slow in the 103 degree heat and a long right to the jaw left him flat on his back, shielding his eyes from the scorching sun. "If Johnson was going to throw that fight, I sure wish he'd have thrown it sooner – it was hotter than hell down there," Willard said.

6th APRIL 1893

After seven hours and 19 minutes, the referee had had enough and called off the lightweight bout between Americans Andy Bowen and Texas Jack Burke at New York's Olympic Club. It is the longest bout in history and many of the 8,000 crowd had fallen asleep. Both fighters were too tired to come out of their corners for the 111th round, prompting the referee's stoppage and declaration of a draw at 3.45am.

6th APRIL 1987

There were genuine concerns for Sugar Ray Leonard's health when he announced his comeback against Marvin Hagler. Leonard had been troubled by a detached retina since 1982 and had not fought for three years before stepping up from welterweight to middleweight. Leonard's boxing on the move earned him a split decision for the

WBC title while Hagler's power only seriously troubled his rival in the ninth round. "You have to remember this is a gambling city," said Hagler after. "Anywhere else in the world I would have got the decision. Leonard fought like a girl." Hagler retired after the fight that grossed $100million.

7th APRIL 2001

Naseem Hamed went from Prince to Pauper when he was left brutally exposed in a unanimous points defeat to Marco Antonio Barrera. In the Sheffield featherweight's highest profile fight, he chose to neglect his training and paid for it against Mexican Barrera, who was deducted a point for irreverently ramming Hamed's head into a ring post. "He was not used to fighting a Mexican who used his own tactics and I beat him at his own game," said Barrera. There was a rematch clause in the fight contract, but Hamed never took it. The defeat was so damaging to former world champion Hamed's career that he only had one more fight. Hamed blamed defeat on not allowing enough time to make the weight.

8th APRIL 2006

Floyd Mayweather Jr's IBF welterweight title fight with Zab Judah was interrupted by a ring riot involving the boxers' family members. Judah was fined $250,000 for punching Mayweather with a low blow and then on the back of the head before joining in the brawl that followed when Mayweather's trainer and uncle, Roger Mayweather, burst into the ring with five seconds left in the tenth round. Judah's father and trainer, Yoel Judah, also climbed through the ropes and threw a punch at Roger Mayweather. Police and security swarmed into the ring and after a five-minute break the world title fight resumed. Mayweather stayed in a neutral corner during the melee and went on to earn a unanimous decision. Roger Mayweather and Yoel Judah were also fined.

9th APRIL 1988

Evander Holyfield unified the world cruiserweight titles by battering Carlos DeLeon on the ropes to force an eighth round stoppage. WBC champion DeLeon finally cracked after being dominated and staggered by IBF-WBA king Holyfield, who was unbeaten at the time. "Man, he looked impressive," said Mike Tyson, who was among the crowd at Caesars Palace. Amid calls that he should face Tyson, this was Holyfield's last fight at cruiserweight before becoming a heavyweight. In two years, Holyfield was undisputed world heavyweight champion, but it would be another eight years before he met Tyson.

10th APRIL 2001

When Robert McCracken announced his retirement from the ring following defeat to Howard Eastman for the European middleweight title, he would never have guessed that he would end up training his opponent in a couple of years. McCracken was stopped in the tenth round by a right uppercut at Wembley Conference Centre by Eastman, who he went on to train as well as Carl Froch and Great Britain's Olympic boxing team.

11th APRIL 1981

Larry Holmes cruised to a comfortable 15-round decision over Jamaican Trevor Berbick, who became the first title challenger to take the WBC world heavyweight champion the full distance. Holmes had stopped his eight previous challengers but could not get rid of Berbick. "He took everything I had and then some," said Holmes. "He just wouldn't go down." Ten years later almost to the day, the pair had a street brawl in Hollywood after one of Holmes's fights. They were twice split up, the second time after Holmes had run over parked cars and jumped legs first on to Berbick.

12th APRIL 1981 & 1989

Joe Louis and Sugar Ray Robinson, two boxing greats, died on this day in 1981 and 1989 respectively. The pair were friends and trailblazers for race relations in America. Robinson was inspired to box after visiting Louis's gym in Detroit as a child and went on to become the best pound-for-pound boxer in history. Louis, for many experts, was the best heavyweight of all time. Louis died of a heart attack aged 66, hours after attending Larry Holmes's world heavyweight title defence against Trevor Berbick. Robinson was a year older when he died at a care home after suffering from Alzheimer's disease and diabetes.

12th APRIL 1997

Oscar De La Hoya earned $10million for becoming a four-weight world champion with his unanimous decision over Pernell Whitaker. It was tough for De La Hoya, who suffered a flash knockdown in the ninth round against the more experienced fighter who like him was a former Olympic gold medallist for America. Whitaker, who got paid $6million, said he was "robbed" and demanded a rematch, but never got one.

13th APRIL 1955

World middleweight champion Carl 'Bobo' Olson belted his way to a ten-round decision over a faded Joey Maxim ahead of his fight against Archie Moore for the world light-heavyweight title. Hawaiian-born Olson floored former world light-heavyweight champion Maxim in the second and ninth rounds of an impressive display in the non-title fight. Maxim had been floored only four times previously in his career and said of Olson: "He hits harder than Moore does." But Moore quickly stopped Olson two months later.

14th APRIL 1979

Victor Galindez won back his WBA light-heavyweight title and got revenge over Mike Rossman after the American retired on his stool before the tenth round. Rossman – known as the Jewish Bomber and the Kosher Butcher – broke his hand in the fifth round but his conqueror had no sympathy. "He's a chicken, a coward and I'll never give him a rematch," said Galindez. "I got a rematch because I deserved it. I won't give him one, because he doesn't deserve it." Two months earlier, Argentine Galindez failed to show for a rematch with Rossman due to a row over the judges.

15th APRIL 1985

The opening three minutes of 'Marvelous' Marvin Hagler against American rival Thomas 'The Hit Man' Hearns for the world middleweight title are hard to beat for entertainment in a boxing ring. By the end of the breathtaking first round after they had furiously hammered each other, Hagler had thrown 82 punches, Hearns 83. That neither had touched down was testament to their superb conditioning. Hagler was bleeding from a cut forehead by

MARVIN HAGLER LOOKS DOWN ON TOMMY HEARNS AFTER FINISHING THEIR CLASSIC CLASH IN 1985

a blow that broke Hearns's hand, and in the second was cut by the right eye. Hearns was on rubbery legs in the second round and when referee Richard Steele asked Hagler if he could still see through the blood, Hagler replied: "I'm not missing him am I?" He then launched a furious assault in the third round to finish off Hearns, who was stopped by Steele after getting up at nine. Hagler landed 50 punches to Hearns's 56 in the first round, a record for middleweights, and Hagler was ahead on two scorecards. Their seven minutes and 52 seconds of intense combat are for some the most thrilling in boxing history.

16th APRIL 1952

Rocky Graziano thought he had Sugar Ray Robinson in trouble in his last world title fight, only to be knocked out seconds later at Chicago Stadium. Graziano – known for his thrilling trilogy with Tony Zale – had gone 21 fights unbeaten in his quest to regain the world middleweight title. Robinson was dominating with his hand speed and movement but was briefly concerned in the third round when Graziano put him down on a knee with a looping right. Robinson quickly sprang to his feet with no count given and seconds later he knocked out Graziano with a right to the jaw. "The count went too fast," said Graziano. "I had the guy but I waited too long to throw the right. Geez, how much an imbecile can a guy be? Just a dumb fighter, me. One second I'm winning, the next I'm hearing 'em count." Graziano would be retired by the end of the year and went on to become a TV personality with his life being made into a film, *Somebody Up There Likes Me*, starring Paul Newman.

17th APRIL 1979

With a minute left of the 12th round, Jim Watt forced a stoppage to capture the vacant WBC world lightweight title from Colombian Alfredo Pitalua. Watt's southpaw right jab put him in control until a two-fisted assault finished off the champion at Kelvin Hall in Glasgow. "I must admit the crowd made it a bit tense," said Watt, who floored Pitalua with a left hook in the seventh round. "You would have to be a zombie not to be affected by their enthusiasm."

18th APRIL 1961

Dave Charnley's late rally from the 13th round was not enough to earn him victory over American Joe 'Old Bones' Brown, who made a tenth defence of his world lightweight title with a debatable points decision at Earls Court, London. The Briton boxed through a mask of blood after being cut above the right eye in the first round and the bridge of his nose was then sliced open in the fifth. Brown, who stopped Charnley on a cut in 1959, returned to Britain in 1963 when the Dartford Destroyer won by sixth round knockout in a third fight.

19th APRIL 2008

Joe Calzaghe was given a shock on his American debut when Bernard Hopkins, then 42, put him down in the first round of their light-heavyweight bout in Las Vegas. The Welshman held on to his unbeaten record by a split decision in what was his penultimate fight before retiring undefeated. "I wasn't given the respect I deserved for beating someone as slippery as Hopkins, who was still beating younger men at nearly 50," said Calzaghe. "What he went on to still achieve after our fight shows you what a legend he is that I beat." Calzaghe had made 21 world title defences of his WBO super-middleweight championship before stepping up a division to face Hopkins, who could not psych out his opponent.

20th APRIL 2002

Floyd Mayweather Jr benefited from a controversial points decision when some thought his undefeated record should have ended in his 28th fight against Mexican José Luis Castillo. The Mexican, who was defending his WBC lightweight title, lost a unanimous decision in Las Vegas but such was the debate over the points verdict that American Mayweather felt obliged to give him a rematch the following December. Mayweather, who became a two-weight world champion by beating Castillo in the first fight, ensured their second meeting was never a close affair, triumphing again on points. Mayweather turned professional after losing on points to Bulgarian Serafim Todorov when the American was 19 in the 1996 Olympic featherweight semi-finals. When this book was published, Mayweather had an unbeaten 48-fight record in the paid ranks.

21st APRIL 1963

Ingemar Johansson, Sweden's former world heavyweight champion, was persuaded it was time to retire when he ended his fight against Briton Brian London slumped against the ropes and in serious trouble. Johansson was dropped heavily by a left hook in the final moments of the 12-round non-title fight and staggered to his feet. The bell rang as the referee was finishing his count and Johansson won the points decision in Stockholm. Johansson, who knocked out Floyd Patterson in 1959 to win the world heavyweight title, went on to become a successful businessman.

22nd APRIL 1995

German Axel Schulz lost the first of three unsuccessful shots at the world heavyweight title when American veteran George Foreman earned a majority points decision. Foreman was then stripped of the title for refusing Schulz a rematch, while the German – known as The Soft Giant – went on to lose points decisions to Frans Botha and Michael Moorer.

22nd APRIL 1995

Lennox Lewis came to regret his acting role in *Ocean's Eleven* as it left him underprepared for little-known Hasim Rahman. London-born Lewis underestimated American Rahman and the altitude of Brakpan, just outside Johannesburg, where his world heavyweight title defence took place. Lewis did not allow enough time to adjust to the altitude and was under-trained; he paid for it when he was caught flush by a right hand after dropping his hands in round five. Later in the year he avenged the defeat with a stunning knockout to regain his titles.

23rd APRIL 1977

Boxing politics insanely contrived that no world titles were on the line when the world's best two bantamweights, Carlos Zarate and Alfonso Zamora, collided in California. But what was at stake was Mexican pride between two bitter rivals who had a combined record of 67-0 (66 KOs) and were former sparring partners. In an explosive encounter, WBA champion Zarate used his height and reach to drop his onrushing foe twice in the fourth round before WBC king Zamora's corner threw in the towel. It ended Zamora's 29-fight unbeaten record and the pair would never meet again.

24th APRIL 2010

A volcanic ash cloud, which had spread from Iceland over most of northern Europe, left Carl Froch and Mikkel Kessler unsure their fight in Denmark would happen until a few days before the fight. The cloud had grounded commercial flights in Europe and WBC super-middleweight champion Froch was late arriving in rural Herning. The pair exchanged shuddering blows in a brutal battle and the last round was an all-out war. Kessler, inspired by his home crowd, out-punched Froch to earn a unanimous decision. Froch blamed his first defeat on his late arrival and would have to wait three years for revenge. Such was the quality of their first fight that 17,000 tickets sold in three hours for the rematch in London.

25th APRIL 2009

It was a thrilling finale to a world title fight – but no major British TV network thought it worth screening live. They missed out as Nottingham's WBC super-middleweight champion Carl Froch produced the grandstand finish he needed to hold on to the belt he had won the previous year. Froch was hoping to impress the American audience on his US debut, but instead was sent to the canvas for the first time in his professional career by Jermain Taylor, a former middleweight world champion, in the third round in Connecticut. "I looked up at the referee and didn't know how I'd got there, so Taylor must have hurt me," said Froch. Trailing on the scorecards, Froch needed a KO to win and he produced it with 14 seconds remaining in the last round by a succession of right hands.

26th APRIL 1985

In only his seventh professional fight, Australian Jeff Fenech won the IBF world bantamweight title by stopping Japan's Satoshi Shingaki. Fenech was just 20, had been professional only six months and would win world titles in three weight divisions.

26th APRIL 2003

James Toney's economical work on the inside was enough to earn him a unanimous points decision and Vassiliy Jirov's IBF world cruiserweight title. It was a classic display from the skilful American in his 70th fight and he put Kazakh Jirov down in the last minute of the fight. It was the first defeat of Jirov's career in his seventh defence as champion.

27th APRIL 1956

Rocky Marciano is the only world heavyweight champion to retire with a perfect unbeaten record. Marciano announced he was hanging up the gloves seven months after knocking out Archie Moore in the ninth round, which extended his record to 49-0, with 43 knockouts. Marciano was 32 when he retired and resisted calls for him to make a comeback against Floyd Patterson and Ingemar Johansson. Born Rocco Francis Marchegiano in Brockton, Massachusetts, he changed his name because ring announcers found it too hard to pronounce. His deadly weapon was his right hand punch, which he called his 'Suzy-Q'. Thirteen years after retiring, Marciano died in a plane crash.

28th APRIL 2012

It seemed like time had finally caught up with 47-year-old Bernard Hopkins when he was outpointed by fellow American Chad Dawson for the WBC light-heavyweight title in Atlantic City. Dawson, who was 18 years younger, had his second round TKO win over Hopkins in 2011 ruled a no-contest because he had thrown his opponent to the canvas. Hopkins was injured and unable to carry on but in the rematch it was Dawson who was left complaining about rough treatment. "My head is hurting from all the head-butts," Dawson said after his victory by majority points decision. "He's a hell of a fighter. But he's a dirty fighter. If you can get through 12 rounds with him, you can get through anything."

29th APRIL 2000

Paul Ingle was glad he went through with his fight against American Junior Jones, after discovering he had to weigh-in on the day of the fight and threatened to pull out. The Yorkshireman, whose IBF featherweight title was not on the line, had to get off the canvas in the ninth round to floor the New Yorker twice in the 11th round before the stoppage at Madison Square Garden. It was the last win of Ingle's career, which would be prematurely ended by head injuries sustained in his next fight.

30th APRIL 2005

James Toney's unanimous points win over John Ruiz was nullified after a post-fight drug test revealed he had used steroids. Toney had won world titles at middleweight and cruiserweight before eating himself up to heavyweight. Ruiz was decked in the seventh round and after losing he announced his retirement, but a month later he would regain his status as WBA champion. Toney was banned after this fight with Ruiz for 90 days and would test positive again for a banned substance two years later.

BOXING
On This Day
History, Facts & Figures
from Every Day of the Year

May

1st MAY 1959

It took Floyd Patterson a surprisingly long time to catch up with Brian London in a world heavyweight title defence that was seen as a warm-up for the American's first fight with Swede Ingemar Johansson the following month. London went down late in the tenth before being finished off early in the 11th by a barrage of body punches and was counted out face down on the canvas. Patterson, who weighed over 20 pounds less than his British challenger, said: "By the time I fight Johansson I will be sharper." Johansson KO'd Patterson in three rounds.

2nd MAY 2015

After over five frustrating years of their mega-money fight not happening, Floyd Mayweather Jr and Manny Pacquiao finally shared the same ring together when they met in front of a star-studded crowd of 16,500 at the MGM Grand in Las Vegas. American Mayweather, 38, and Filipino Pacquiao, 36, had won (WBC/WBA/IBF/WBO) world titles at five and seven weight divisions respectively and were the best boxers of their generation. It may have been the richest fight ever for three world welterweight titles, making more than $500m, but it was not the best fight ever. And Mayweather's unanimous (118-110, 116-112, 116-112) points win did not make him more popular. Mayweather spent fight week insisting he was TBE – The Best Ever – but few were left believing he actually was after he contained Pacquiao. It was a conservative and defensively masterful performance by Mayweather, who used his reach advantage to land jab after jab. Despite his dominance, unbeaten Mayweather did not take any chances by looking for the KO finish as he moved, boxed and countered his way to 48-0. Pacquiao blamed a torn rotator cuff in his right shoulder, sustained in training which later required surgery, for leaving him unusually subdued in his attacks. "I'm fighting in September then it's time for me to hang it up," said Mayweather, who made at least $180million to Pacquiao's $120m.

3rd MAY 2003

Yori Boy Campas was a former champion but a faded force when he faced WBA-WBC light-middleweight champion Oscar De La Hoya and his corner had seen enough of the one-sided beating before the end of the seventh round. Victory for De La Hoya set up a rematch with Sugar Shane Mosley.

FLOYD MAYWEATHER JR AND MANNY PACQUIAO IN THEIR 2015 MEGA-MONEY BOUT

4th MAY 1982

Charlie Magri's career seemed ruined after his second defeat in eight months to a Mexican. The Londoner, who was European flyweight champion at the time, was ahead on points when Joe Torres caught him with a looping left at the start of the ninth round. Magri, born in Tunisia but raised in east London, never recovered and after two counts the referee stopped the fight. Magri was written off after the defeat at Wembley Arena, but less than a year later he had got revenge over Torres and become world flyweight champion. On the undercard of Magri's loss to Torres was a 20-year-old heavyweight called Frank Bruno, who notched up his fourth professional win.

5th MAY 1925

The 10,105 crowd at Madison Square Garden booed at the end of the last fight on its second site, Sid Terris's dour 12-round points decision over Johnny Dundee. Among those who had come to say goodbye to the famous fight venue was Jack Dempsey, the reigning world heavyweight champion. Before the fight, ring announcer Joe Humphreys delivered a melancholy eulogy (without a microphone): "Farewell to thee, o temple of fistiana. Farewell to thee, o sweet Miss Diana..." On top of the building and 347ft above street level was a golden statue of the Greek goddess Diana but despite looking the part the venue – designed by architect Stanford White – had failed to make money and after the anti-climactic Terris-Dundee bout its doors were shut for demolition the next day. The third MSG – owned by promoter Tex Rickard – ran from 1925 to 1968 and the current Garden is the fourth incarnation.

6th MAY 1920

Mike O'Dowd complained about the referee's decision after unheralded Johnny Wilson – whose real name was Giovanni Francesco Panica – captured his world middleweight title on points in Boston. New Yorker Wilson's southpaw stance troubled O'Dowd, who was dropped in the second round by a left to the jaw. In a rematch a year later, Wilson prevailed on a split decision and held the title until losing it to Harry Greb in 1923.

7th MAY 2005

In a scarcely believable turnaround, Diego Corrales stopped José Luis Castillo moments after twice being floored in the tenth round. There are not many fights that can match this world lightweight title unification clash for a dramatic end. Castillo, the Mexican two-time WBC champion, looked set to win a classic toe-to-toe encounter against the American. It was dirty at times, like a street fight to the death, and by the tenth round Corrales could hardly see Castillo through the slits of his eyes such was the swelling. Corrales had a slight lead but was then sunk by a left hook and was on spaghetti legs when he got up. After being decked for a second time, Corrales intentionally spat his gum shield out to buy more time for his head to clear and when the fight resumed, he threw a desperate overhand right that scrambled Castillo's senses. Castillo was rendered an immobile target against the ropes until the slaughter was stopped. An inevitable rematch followed five months later and after Castillo weighed in over the stipulated weight, he stopped Corrales in four rounds. In 2007, Corrales was killed in a motorbike accident.

8th MAY 1993

Gerald McClellan won the battle of two middleweight bangers when he took out Julian Jackson in the fifth round for the WBC belt. McClellan's last six opponents had failed to make it past the second round and once again his power proved decisive. Yet the stoppage came as a surprise with the champion ahead on two of the scorecards. American McClellan caught Jackson with a right and then dropped him with an explosive left hook. Jackson, of the Virgin Islands, got up to be stopped on his feet. In the rematch almost exactly a year later, Jackson lasted just 83 seconds with the G Man.

9th MAY 1970

Mexican Vicente Saldivar regained the world featherweight title in Rome when he unanimously outpointed Australian Johnny Famechon over 15 rounds, after flooring the champion in the 13th round. Saldivar had dominated the division since 1964 but his second reign as champion, after nearly two years "retired", was short-lived: he lost the belt in a first defence later in the year.

10th MAY 1989

Herol Graham's late onslaught was not enough in his vacant WBA world middleweight title fight with Mike McCallum, who took the split points decision. McCallum was given a count in round five, despite looking to have slipped on some spilt water, but it did not hinder his progress and he wobbled the British fighter in the ninth. What proved costly for skilful British boxer Graham was having a point deducted in round eight for shoving his Jamaican opponent into a ring post. Two of the three judges had it 115-114 and 117-114 to McCallum.

11th MAY 1922

Londoner Ted 'Kid' Lewis, the former world welterweight champion, was past his best when he challenged world light-heavyweight champion Georges Carpentier. But the 11-stone Lewis boldly thought that a victory over Carpentier would lead to a lucrative fight for the world heavyweight title. The Frenchman, who was two stones heavier, had lost to world heavyweight champion Jack Dempsey only the previous year and was one of the biggest stars of the sport. Lewis's plan of using Carpentier as a stepping stone did not work out as the Frenchman knocked him out in the first round after the Londoner dropped his hands when the referee called for the fighters to break for holding.

12th MAY 2001

Felix Trinidad became a three-weight world champion with a fifth round destruction of American William Joppy at Madison Square Garden. Joppy was down in the first, fourth and fifth rounds as he became the latest victim of the impressive Puerto Rican. "I've never been hit like that before," said Joppy, who was on legs of jelly for much of the fight after being nailed by a left hook in the first round. Trinidad had already beaten the likes of Fernando Vargas, Oscar De La Hoya and Pernell Whitaker and claiming Joppy's WBA middleweight belt set up a fight with Bernard Hopkins later in the year. Three world titles were on the line when Hopkins became the first person to stop Trinidad.

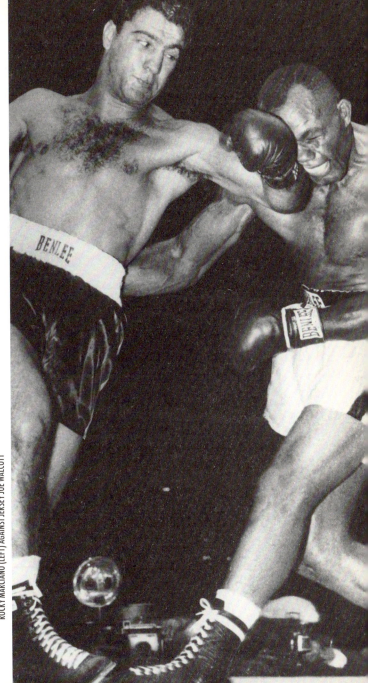

ROCKY MARCIANO (LEFT) AGAINST JERSEY JOE WALCOTT

13th MAY 1989

Julio Cesar Chavez's masterful display left Roger Mayweather so sickened that the American quit after ten rounds complaining of stomach cramps. Chavez became a three-weight world champion after capturing the WBC light-welterweight title and by now was the sport's biggest star. Chavez, Mexico's greatest boxer, had dominated and was ahead by six and seven rounds on the judges' scorecards. The win over Mayweather was one of six fights for the Mexican legend in 1989. Roger Mayweather, who Chavez also stopped in two rounds in 1985, went on to train his nephew Floyd Mayweather Jr, who won world titles at five weight divisions.

14th MAY 1957

"Who do you want to fight next?" Terry Downes was asked in the dressing room after his third professional fight against the then unknown Liverpool-based Nigerian Dick Tiger. "The silly ****er who made that match," replied Londoner Downes, who was floored and then stopped in the sixth round by Tiger. Both would go on to win the world middleweight title, although global glory did not seem likely for Downes at the time. "I thought 'Hello, Tiger looks a lot bigger than me'. But it was because I was on the floor looking up at him," said Downes.

15th MAY 1953

Rocky Marciano was at his vicious best when he disposed of Jersey Joe Walcott in just two minutes and 25 seconds at the Chicago Stadium. Marciano had beaten Walcott in the 13th round for the world heavyweight title in his previous fight but this was a lot quicker. And it was too quick for Walcott, who complained of a fast count after being dumped on his backside by a right uppercut. "I thought the count only reached eight," said 39-year-old former champion Walcott, a father of six children. Marciano's ninth successive stoppage win was his first world title defence. American Marciano's reign would become one of the most famous in boxing history but Walcott's was over with this defeat. Walcott, whose real name was Arnold Raymond Cream, lost two world title fights to Joe Louis and two to Ezzard Charles as well. He then beat Charles to become the oldest boxer to win the world heavyweight title aged 37 years, 168 days in a record that stood until 1994.

16th MAY 1955

Rocky Marciano was allowed to violate practically every rule in the book during a foul-filled ninth round win against brave British challenger Don Cockell. The world heavyweight champion was guilty of throwing kidney punches, punching after the bell, using his elbows, cutting Cockell on the forehead with a butt in the fourth round, hitting Cockell when he was down and frequently landing low blows. Marciano was allowed to do all this without one warning from the referee Frank Brown, who stepped in to stop the slaughter in the ninth round after Cockell had risen from a count of eight. "Marciano was a bit deaf when it came to hearing the bell," said Cockell about being illegally hit following the end of some rounds in San Francisco. "I don't think I hit anyone else any more or often as I did Cockell," said Marciano after his penultimate fight.

17th MAY 1966

Randy Turpin, nearly 15 years after beating Sugar Ray Robinson for the world middleweight title, shot and killed himself upstairs from his café in Leamington. He was 37. The former boxer unloaded two bullets into his chest and head, with 17-month-old daughter Carmen also suffering two gunshot wounds. Carmen survived and her dad's death was ruled as suicide at an inquest after he had become depressed and stressed at an unpaid tax bill of £15,000.

18th MAY 2002

Arturo Gatti and Micky Ward have become synonymous with each other because of their thrilling trilogy. Round nine of their first encounter in Connecticut is one of the best in boxing history. The punishment both were able to absorb was astonishing and yet they both kept marching forward. Gatti, based in New Jersey after being born in Italy and brought up in Canada, sunk to one knee from a left to the body but just as Ward, from Massachusetts, looked to be on the brink of a stoppage back came Gatti. A world title was not even on the line and Ward, who at 37 was seven years older, got the ten round majority decision. All three fights went to points and all three were brilliant brawls; Gatti won the series 2-1 nearly a year later.

19th MAY 1995

Colombian Jimmy Garcia, aged 23, died of brain damage 13 days after sustaining head injuries in his 11th round stoppage defeat to Gabriel Ruelas for the WBC world super-featherweight title in Las Vegas. Ruelas got up from a count before being stopped in the 11th round and less than half an hour later he was being taken to hospital in an ambulance with a blood clot on the brain. Brain surgery could not reverse the damage and he was in a coma until the life support machine was turned off. Mexican Ruelas considered retiring after Garcia's death before resuming his career.

20th MAY 1983

Larry Holmes was fortunate to extend his unbeaten record to 43-0 after a dubious split points decision over fellow American Tim Witherspoon at the outdoor Dunes Hotel in Las Vegas. Witherspoon, 25, was a 6-1 outside bet and with only 15 fights experience but he rocked the WBC heavyweight champion, who was making a 15th defence, in the ninth round. Yet it was enough to beat Holmes, 33, who blamed his performance on being too light. "I think I left a lot of my strength in the bathroom," Holmes said after weighing in at 213 pounds. Holmes earned $2.1million – nearly ten times more than Witherspoon.

21st MAY 1966

Henry Cooper's face was once again reduced to a bloody mask, crushing his and Britain's hopes. The Londoner had been hoping to get revenge on Muhammad Ali, the world heavyweight champion, but the outcome was similar to the first time they met with blood spurting from Cooper's face. Cooper, 32, was stopped by a jagged gash across his left eyebrow in the sixth round in front of 41,000 at Highbury, home of Arsenal Football Club. The 24-year-old's blows were accurate but Cooper's valiant effort was prematurely ended and he would never fight for the world title again. In their first fight three years previously, Ali – then Cassius Clay – stopped Cooper in five rounds on a cut at Wembley Stadium. In Clay's last bout before taking on heavyweight champ Sonny Liston for the world title, Cooper knocked him down in the fourth round before the American's quick hands opened up a grotesque cut over Cooper's left eye.

22nd MAY 1993

Roy Jones Jr captured his first world title when he scored a convincing points victory over fellow American Bernard Hopkins for the vacant IBF world middleweight title in Washington. Jones overcame an early hand injury in what was the first world title fight for both boxers who would go on to become two stars of recent times. Jones triumphed 116-112 on all three scorecards and a year later had stepped up a division. Hopkins would not lose for another 13 years but would have to wait 17 years to get revenge over Jones, who by then was a shell of his former self.

23rd MAY 1922

Harry Greb overwhelmed Gene Tunney in the latter half of the 15-round light-heavyweight bout to earn a points win and inflict the future world heavyweight champion's only ever defeat. Tunney was cut above both eyes and was hospitalised by the first of five bouts with Greb. Tunney won three of their fights, some of which were disputed decisions, and there was a draw. The pair could not have been more different in boxing styles or personalities. Greb was a dirty brawler, heavy drinker and womaniser; Tunney was a scientific boxer, a lover of Shakespeare and friends with playwright George Bernard Shaw. Greb later had a three-year reign as world middleweight champion (1923-26) but this battering of Tunney was his finest hour. It is thought that he fought nine of his world title fights while blind in one eye. Greb died the same year he lost the title after a nose operation.

24th MAY 1968

Bob Foster became the only man to knock out Dick Tiger when he captured the world light-heavyweight title in New York. Nigeria-born Tiger was a two-weight world champion and seven inches smaller than American Foster. Tiger was flattened by a left hook and was counted out in the fourth round for the only time in his career, which would be over two years later before his death in 1971 through liver cancer.

25th MAY 1965

It was called the phantom punch – a right hand punch that never was – which finished off Sonny Liston in his rematch with Muhammad Ali, who had changed his name from Cassius Clay, in Lewiston, Maine.

Only 2,500 had turned up to see the fight as many were put off by the suspicion of a fix. The confusing fight lasted just 60 seconds and many believed Liston took a dive for the Mob who would have cashed in on betting on a first round win for Ali. When Liston went down, referee Jersey Joe Walcott – the former world heavyweight champion – failed to take up the count and when Liston got to his feet the timekeeper, *Ring* magazine editor Nat Fleischer, told him that Liston had already been counted out. As Liston lay on his back looking up, Ali looked down at him screaming "Get up, get up". The crowd chanted "Fix, Fix, Fix" as the fight was waved off. Liston's career never recovered but Ali's would continue on an upward trajectory as he transcended the sport. There has never been a more famous or charismatic boxer, or sportsman, than Ali. The gloves worn by Ali in this fight were sold for $956,000 at auction in February 2015.

26th MAY 2000

US president Bill Clinton signed the Muhammad Ali Boxing Reform Act, aimed at flushing out corruption from boxing. Its goal was: "To reform unfair and anticompetitive practices in the professional boxing industry". Among other things, it placed a one-year limit on the length of a boxer's contract with a promoter and financial relationships between promoters and managers, stopping managers or promoters from making improper payments to governing bodies.

27th MAY 1995

Henry Maske made a seventh defence of his IBF world light-heavyweight title with a unanimous points decision over fellow German Graciano Rocchigiani. Unbeaten Maske was a huge star in Germany after winning Olympic middleweight gold for East Germany in 1988. After the unification of Germany, Maske turned professional in 1990 and three years later was world champion. He won a rematch later in 1995 with Rocchigiani but lost his title in an 11th defence against Virgil Hill the following year and then retired (before a meaningless comeback 11 years later).

28th MAY 1917

Benny Leonard was crowned world lightweight champion after flooring Freddie Welsh three times in round nine before the fight was stopped. It had taken three fights for New Yorker Leonard, 21, to get the better of the Welshman, who was ten years older, and he would defend the title six times until he retired as undefeated champion in 1925 (he made a comeback nearly seven years later but never fought for the title again after vacating it). By the time he fought Leonard for a third time, Welsh was regularly enjoying the nightlife on Broadway and Leonard was too fast and fresh for him. Welsh's real name was Frederick Thomas and lived in Pontypridd, Wales, before he relocated to America where he took up boxing. The Leonard loss was the start of a downward spiral for Welsh, who lost his money on the Wall Street crash.

29th MAY 1933

It had taken Irish-Canadian Jimmy McLarnin five years to get a second world welterweight title shot after losing to Sammy Mandell, but his bout with Young Corbett III only lasted two minutes 37 seconds and was a big upset. Corbett had been floored twice before McLarnin left him out on his feet to prompt the stoppage. One day short of a year later, the Belfast Spider – as McLarnin was known – lost the belt on a split points decision in a first defence to Barney Ross in front of 60,000. It was the first of three world welterweight title fights with Ross, who won the trilogy 2-1. McLarnin was born in Hillsborough, County Down but his family moved to Vancouver when he was three.

30th MAY 1961

Belfast plumber Johnny Caldwell captured the European version of the world bantamweight title by upsetting the odds against Algerian Alphonse Halimi. Caldwell won a 15-round decision at Wembley but he entered the fight known as a flyweight. He was British flyweight champion and had never fought above 115 pounds. At 116 pounds, Caldwell was well inside the bantamweight limit but his energy saw him outpunch the champion and floor him in the last round. Caldwell won a rematch and his career was finished by 1965.

31st MAY 2003

Audley Harrison, never shy to extol his questionable qualities, was feeling pleased with himself after a second round win over Mathew

CARL FROCH CELEBRATES HIS KNOCKOUT OF GEORGE GROVES IN 2014

Ellis that he hoped would stop the criticism of his slow-moving career. The 2000 Olympic gold medallist was halfway through a TV interview when it was interrupted by a riot, later investigated by police. Herbie Hide, a former holder of the WBO world heavyweight title, was standing nearby while Londoner Harrison was being interviewed live on BBC TV and allegedly pushed a woman off a chair. Pushing and shoving followed before Hide fled the scene. Chairs and punches were thrown before Norwich hot-head Hide ran through the York Hall in Bethnal Green. Hide said: "I never pushed anybody. I was wearing a £3,000 Armani suit and an £85,000 watch. If I had come for a fight I would not be wearing those things. They broke my watch and battered my BMW when I tried to drive away afterwards."

31st MAY 2014

For Carl Froch, the huge right hand that left George Groves in a heap in front of 80,000 fans at Wembley and millions watching on television was undoubtedly the most satisfying punch of his career. Groves had verbally teased and provoked Froch for the past year in the build-up to their two WBA-IBF world super-middleweight title fights, but he had now silenced the Londoner for good. "That's the best punch I've thrown in my life," Froch said. "It's one of the most satisfying nights of my life because I've had George Groves in my earhole for a year." After Groves had claimed he had been stopped prematurely in the ninth round of their first fight in November 2013, which the Londoner was winning on the judges' scorecards after flooring Froch in the first round, there was huge public demand for a rematch which attracted Britain's biggest post-Second World War boxing attendance. After a nervous start, Nottingham's three-time world champion Froch relaxed and once he had Groves trapped on the ropes, threw a straight right that landed flush on the jaw to ensure there were no doubts over the outcome this time around. Groves managed to pull himself up but the fight was waved off and he had no complaints.

BOXING
On This Day
History, Facts & Figures
from Every Day of the Year

June

1st JUNE 1964

Ismael Laguna was left cursing the judges after they returned a unanimous ten-round decision against him and in favour of local hero Vicente Saldivar amid an intimidating atmosphere generated by 10,000 fans in a bullring in Tijuana, Mexico. It was a pivotal fight for Saldivar since he would challenge for and win the WBA-WBC world featherweight titles in his next fight. Laguna, from Panama, decided to step up to lightweight where he won the world title the following year.

2nd JUNE 1913

Britain's first world flyweight champion Sid Smith relinquished the title after being knocked out in the 11th round by Bill Ladbury in a catchweight bout between the two south Londoners at The Ring, Blackfriars. Smith, from Bermondsey, had dominated until the seventh round when local rival Ladbury, from Deptford, scored four knockdowns. Smith was spilled on the canvas four more times in the tenth round and numerous times in the 11th before the massacre was stopped. Smith had only won the title from Eugene Criqui in Paris two months previously while Ladbury would lose the belt in a first defence before being killed during the First World War.

3rd JUNE 1979

Carlos Zarate could not believe it when it was announced he had lost by split decision to fellow Mexican Lupe Pintor, who looked stunned to have got the verdict and then left sheepishly from the Las Vegas ring with the WBC bantamweight title. Two judges scored it 143-142 for Pintor, who was floored in the fourth, while the other saw it 147-133 for Zarate. The decision disgusted Zarate so much that he did not box for another seven years.

3rd JUNE 2006

After becoming the biggest world heavyweight champion in history, Russian 7ft and 23-stone giant Nikolai Valuev swatted Jamaican Owen Beck in three rounds in Germany. Known as the Beast from the East, Valuev dropped Beck with a right uppercut to leave veteran promoter Don King excitedly talking about conquering America following this first defence of the WBA title. Valuev's questionable

ability did not dampen King's enthusiasm. One newspaper reported: "King has found his Kong".

4th JUNE 2005

Ricky Hatton announced himself on the world stage by sending Kostya Tszyu into retirement and winning his IBF light-welterweight title. The Manchester boxer thrilled 22,000 of his home fans with a tireless display that ground down Russia-born Australia-based Tszyu, whose trainer Johnny Lewis pulled him out before the start of the 12th round. Tszyu – at 34, nine years older than his challenger – entered the fight as favourite but could not contend with Hatton's relentless attack. "If I can be half the champion Tszyu is, I'll be doing very well," said Hatton, who was known as Ricky Fatton for ballooning in weight between fights. Defeat to Hatton was just the second setback in ten years for Tszyu, most of which time was spent as a world champion. For Hatton, it never got better than this moment but this fight launched his career in America where he fought the likes of Jose Luis Castillo, Paulie Malignaggi, Manny Pacquiao and Floyd Mayweather Jr.

5th JUNE 2004

Oscar De La Hoya was saved from an embarrassing defeat by a controversial points win over Felix Sturm. The German looked fresher and outworked the American, who got away with his pallid performance courtesy of a unanimous decision of 115-113 on all three cards. But Compubox stats told a different story: Sturm landed 234 punches to De La Hoya's 188 punches. De La Hoya's celebrations were muted after he lifted the WBO middleweight title in Las Vegas. "What can I say? I stepped in the ring, and 'boom' – nothing," said De La Hoya. "It was a very close fight, let's put it that way." De La Hoya needed the win to set up a unification title fight with Bernard Hopkins.

6th JUNE 1988

Iran Barkley looked doomed until he turned around his fight with Thomas Hearns in the third round and stopped him. Barkley was cut above both eyes and heading for defeat when he threw everything he had at WBC middleweight champion Hearns. Barkley knocked

Hearns on to his back with two big rights to the chin and the Detroit boxer barely beat the count. When he got up, Barkley tore into him to prompt the stoppage. At the time, only Sugar Ray Leonard and Marvin Hagler had stopped The Hitman.

7th JUNE 1989

Dave 'Boy' McAuley captured a version of the world flyweight title at the third attempt when he outpointed fellow Briton Duke McKenzie at Wembley Arena. Despite a 15-month ring exile, the Northern Irish cook served up an impressive display to earn the IBF belt with a 117-113, 115-113 and 115-113 points triumph to end McKenzie's unbeaten record.

8th JUNE 1985

In front of a record 18 million TV viewers in the UK, Barry McGuigan lifted the WBA world featherweight title after a points victory over Eusebio Pedroza at Loftus Road, the home of QPR Football Club in west London. McGuigan's appeal was not simply down to his exquisite boxing, but his brave stance during the Troubles in Northern Ireland. McGuigan was from the border town of Clones in the Republic of Ireland but based in Belfast. McGuigan, a Catholic, married a Protestant and he became a hero for both communities. When he fought, the troubled streets went quiet as part of an informal ceasefire. "Leave the fighting to McGuigan," was the slogan and McGuigan rose to the occasion in his biggest fight with an indefatigable display against the ageing champion from Panama.

8th JUNE 2002

Those that were clinging to the belief that Mike Tyson could dominate boxing again like he did in the eighties were made to think again as the former world heavyweight champion folded in eight rounds to Lennox Lewis. Tyson did not offer much to back up his old pseudonym of 'Baddest Man on the Planet', but this bout cemented Lewis's status as the best heavyweight of his era. The fight significantly matched two of the best heavyweights of the last two decades of the 20th century. After biting Lewis at a pre-fight press conference, Tyson embraced his conqueror and kissed Lewis's mum in the ring after the fight.

9th JUNE 2012

Filipino Manny Pacquiao lost for the first time in seven years when he was victim of an outrageous split points decision defeat to American Tim Bradley for the WBO welterweight title. "I have both guys, and I'll make a lot of money in the rematch, but it's ridiculous," said promoter Bob Arum. "It's incompetence. Nobody who knows anything about boxing could have Bradley ahead in the fight." Pac Man, who landed 253 punches to 159 for Bradley, won a rematch two years later.

10th JUNE 1948

Tony Zale lived up to his word and stopped Rocky Graziano in the third round to regain the world middleweight title. Zale, eight years older than the champion, predicted he would finish his rival in three and he did in the last of three brutal bouts between the two Americans. Graziano was nailed by some huge blows but just would not go down before a swinging left hook knocked him off his feet in the third. Graziano hauled himself up but was semi-conscious as Zale unloaded more sickening blows until a right to the body followed by a left hook to the jaw left Graziano flat on his back, his senses scrambled. But the trilogy had taken its toll on Zale – known as the Man of Steel – and he was stopped by Frenchman Marcel Cerdan in his next and final fight. Graziano claimed that for years after he was woken in cold sweats by nightmares of him being back in the ring with Zale.

11th JUNE 1982

Larry Holmes called Gerry Cooney the "Great White Dope" before his 12th WBC heavyweight title defence but his fellow American was no pushover. Holmes, who had been champion since beating Ken Norton in 1978, made a good start when he floored his challenger in the second. But Cooney recovered to keep the fight close until he had three points deducted for low blows and was then stopped as he tired in the 13th round. "He was scared stiff of me but what did Marlon Brando's brother say in *On the Waterfront*? 'It wasn't your night, kid'. It wasn't my night."

12th JUNE 1989

Eight years after their first brilliant fight, old rivals Sugar Ray Leonard and Thomas Hearns fought to a points draw. It was not the revenge Hearns had wanted and once again he was left feeling aggrieved. Hearns felt he had been stopped prematurely in their first fight as rival world welterweight champions. This time, with two super-middleweight titles on the line, Hearns floored Leonard in the third and 11th rounds. Leonard had his moments and almost knocked out Hearns in the fifth round. "I just didn't have that magic," said Leonard, 33.

13th JUNE 1935

James J Braddock's rags to riches story earned him the nickname Cinderella Man, whose life was turned into a film starring Russell Crowe, as he punched his way from penniless journeyman to world heavyweight champion with a 15-round decision over Max Baer in New York. It was writer Damon Runyon who gave Braddock his famous moniker for resurrecting a career from that of a losing journeyman, who worked on the docks while injured, to champion and folk hero in Depression-hit America. The general public lapped up the human life story of the Irish-American's struggle to keep his family warm and fed in New Jersey. But Baer was heavily fancied to win their fight because of his fearsome reputation. In 1930, Frankie Campbell died a day after his fifth round defeat to Baer because his brain had been "knocked completely loose from his skull". A year later Baer lost on points to Tommy Loughran and watching at the back of the hall that night after boxing on the undercard was Braddock, who used Loughran's tactics as a blueprint to beat Baer.

14th JUNE 1982

Young Ali, whose real name was Asymin Mustapha, collapsed moments after getting out of the ring after suffering a knockout defeat to Irish prospect Barry McGuigan at a dinner show in London. The Nigerian boxer, who had been knocked out in the sixth round, was taken to hospital and remained in a coma for six months until dying back in his homeland on December 13th. The post-mortem revealed Ali had an exceptionally thin skull. A tearful McGuigan would dedicate his world featherweight title triumph to Ali three years later.

15th JUNE 1984

Thomas Hearns made it look easy when he demolished Roberto Duran in two rounds for the WBC light-middleweight title. At the end of the first round, Duran stumbled to a neutral corner after two visits to the canvas. Duran fell face first to the canvas in the second round from a right to the jaw. "That was the fight that most affected me because when I got to Panama City the police grabbed me and they put me in jail because I had lost that fight," said Duran, who suffered depression after losing to Hearns and was out of the ring for 18 months.

16th JUNE 1983

Unbeaten Billy Collins Jr sustained career-ending injuries at the hands of Luis Resto's illegally tampered gloves and less than a year later was dead, aged 22. Resto won a unanimous ten-round decision but when Collins Jr's father shook Resto's hand after the fight, he realised the gloves did not have enough padding in them. Resto's trainer Carlos 'Panama' Lewis had not only removed padding from the gloves but dipped his fighter's hand wraps in plaster of Paris, turning his fists into wrecking balls. The result was Collins Jr's face was left grotesquely swollen and he suffered a torn iris and permanently blurred vision. Collins Jr, 22, was killed in March 1984 when he crashed his car while under the influence of alcohol and there were theories it was suicide after he had grown depressed at the end of his boxing career. Resto and Lewis were both jailed.

17th JUNE 2000

Oscar De La Hoya allowed a points lead to slip from his grasp as Shane Mosley pulled off an upset to win the WBC welterweight title by split decision at the Staples Center in Los Angeles. Most expected De La Hoya, a world champion in four weight divisions, to triumph over his fellow American and by round eight he led on two scorecards. But De La Hoya tired and Mosley decisively began landing more blows.

18th JUNE 1941

Joe Louis stopped Billy Conn in the 13th round in what he regarded as the toughest fight of his reign as world heavyweight champion. The Brown Bomber had left a trail of destruction behind him since winning the title in 1937 and Conn was expected to be another contributor to the Louis collection of "Bum of the Month". In the 12th, Conn had the temerity to give Louis serious problems when a series of left hooks staggered the champion. Consumed by confidence, Conn looked for the KO blow in the 13th but left himself an open target. As Conn threw a left hook, Louis launched a short right, followed by a series of blows that sent Conn to the canvas. Two of the three judges had Conn ahead at the stoppage. "I thought I had him and I simply couldn't do anything else but go after him," said Conn. "Then it happened. What's the point in being Irish if you can't be dumb."

19th JUNE 1936

Max Schmeling stopped Joe Louis in the 12th round of an upset that would make their second fight two years later the biggest rematch in boxing history. The German may have been a former world champion (1930-31) but he was still a 10-1 outsider to beat the unbeaten young American who was steamrolling his way towards the world heavyweight title. But Schmeling repeatedly caught Louis with an overhand right and when the American went down for a third time in the 12th, he did not get up at the Yankee Stadium in New York.

20th JUNE 1942

Freddie Mills, a former Bournemouth milkman and sergeant in the RAF, captured the British light-heavyweight title by stopping Cornishman Len Harvey at White Hart Lane. With barrage balloons hovering overhead at Tottenham Hotspur's ground, Mills – then 22 – delighted the 30,000 crowd when he put his opponent, who was 12 years older than him, through the ropes with a left hook. The fight was held during the day because of the night-time blackout during the Second World War.

20th JUNE 1980

Roberto Duran had nothing but contempt for Sugar Ray Leonard and when the American put his hands in the air at the end of their world welterweight title fight, the Panama hero lashed out at him and started beating his chest. Macho-man Duran thought he deserved victory after drawing the skilful Leonard – 1976 Olympic gold medallist – into a brawl in Montreal. It was the sort of fight that appealed to Duran, who earned a unanimous points decision in the first of three fights between the rivals.

21st JUNE 2003

Vitali Klitschko's face looked like it had been through a cheese grater in Lennox Lewis's last fight. Klitschko, who had stepped in at ten days' notice as a replacement for Canadian Kirk Johnson, was winning on all scorecards when he was stopped by a hideous cut on doctor's orders after six rounds in Los Angeles. The Ukrainian could not see out of his left eye due to a jagged gash beneath the eyebrow caused by a right hand in the third round. Lewis, more than six years older than his challenger, had looked slow and heavy in his WBC heavyweight title defence and announced his retirement in February 2004.

22nd JUNE 1938

Never has a fight had so much political symbolism as the time Joe Louis subjected Max Schmeling to 124 seconds of pain and torture in defence of his world heavyweight title. In a fight that had worldwide appeal and transcended sport, Louis represented the American Dream while Schmeling was an unwilling tool of the Nazi propaganda machine one year before the start of the Second World War. Louis, 24, was driven to avenge his 12th round defeat to Schmeling in 1936 and brilliantly overwhelmed his 32-year-old opponent. Louis seemed possessed as he unloaded a right to the jaw early on and after more unanswered blows, a stunned Schmeling was given a count. The ever-dignified Louis maintained his impassive mask, even when he was reducing Schmeling to a screeching wreck as a body blow displaced one of the bones in his spinal column.

23rd JUNE 1986

Barry McGuigan fried in the 110 degree heat of Las Vegas as he lost an agonising points decision unanimously (143-142, 143-139, 142-141) to American Steve Cruz. In the third defence of the Irishman's WBA world featherweight title, McGuigan just could not cope with the outdoor venue's baking heat at Caesars Palace. McGuigan was

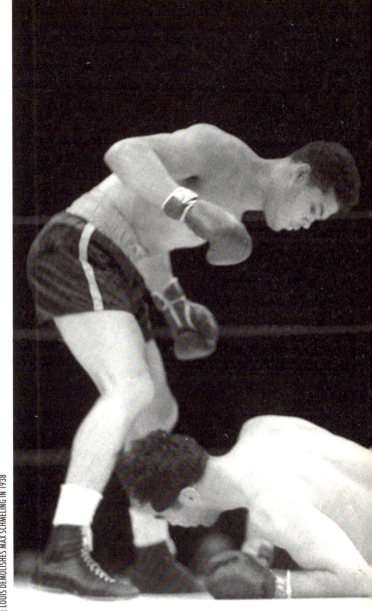

JOE LOUIS DEMOLISHES MAX SCHMELING IN 1938

floored in the tenth but then bravely gave everything in rounds 13 and 14 to lead on points. There was not much in Cruz's pitter-patter combinations but it was enough to put a drained McGuigan down twice in the last round. Along with a point deducted in the 12th round for persistent holding by McGuigan, the last round – scored 10-7 by two judges who gave the fight to Cruz by a point – proved decisive.

24th JUNE 1989

Jeff Harding recovered from an early siege to halt Dennis Andries in the 12th round after a brutal brawl in Atlantic City. Australian Harding, 24, was 11 years younger and needed the stoppage as Andries was ahead on all three scorecards at the time. Harding, who was a late substitute opponent for Guyana-born UK-based Andries, had a torrid time early on and had been cut and floored by the fifth round. But Andries faded badly in the 11th and looked exhausted after being floored for a second time and it was stopped.

25th JUNE 1917

Ted 'Kid' Lewis met American rival Jack Britton for the fourth time in 38 days and just 11 days after their last encounter when the world welterweight title was on the line. Londoner Lewis got the 20-round decision and held on to the title until losing to Britton in their next encounter nine months later. They met 20 times from 1915 to 1921, with Britton winning the series 4-3 (there was one draw and 12 no decisions). It was the only world title fight between the pair that Lewis won.

25th JUNE 1952

In the only time Sugar Ray Robinson failed to finish a fight, Joey Maxim won when his Sugarness retired at the end of 13 rounds. Robinson was suffering from heat exhaustion, which had also claimed referee Ruby Goldstein who had to be replaced in the tenth round. "He complained about the heat, but what did he think I had, air conditioning?" said world light-heavyweight champion Maxim. Robinson, who had stepped up from middleweight, announced he had retired in December 1952, only to return in 1955.

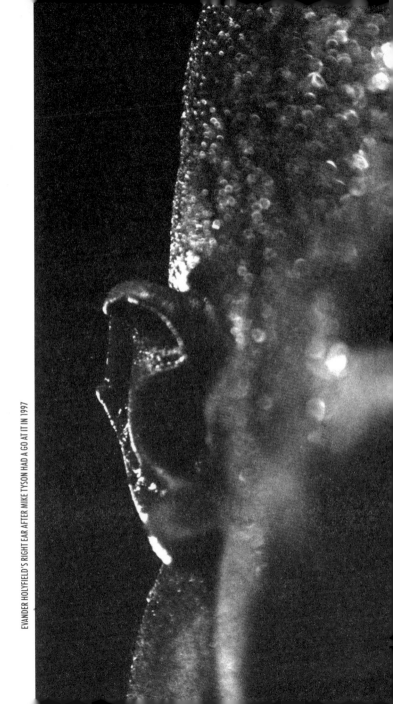

EVANDER HOLYFIELD'S RIGHT EAR AFTER MIKE TYSON HAD A GO AT IT IN 1997

26th JUNE 1972

Ken Buchanan had one of his testicles split in two by a low blow from the young, maniacal Roberto Duran at Madison Square Garden. Duran was heading for a wide points victory (he led 9-2-1, 9-3 and 8-3-1 on the scorecards at the end of the 12th) when late in the 13th his street instinct brought a controversial conclusion to the world lightweight title fight he was destined to win anyway. As referee Johnny LoBianco tried to grab Duran and pull him away at the sound of the bell, the Panamanian unloaded a low uppercut between Buchanan's legs. A boxer is allowed up to five minutes to recover from a low blow, but LoBianco did not deem it low and waved the fight off within a minute with Buchanan writhing in agony.

27th JUNE 1890

Canadian-born George Dixon became the first black world champion when he beat Englishman Nunc Wallace for the bantamweight title in London. Both touched down in an explosive fourth round before Dixon stopped Wallace in the 18th at the Pelican Club in Soho to be recognised as world bantamweight champion. After returning to America, Dixon soon put on weight and relinquished the title.

28th JUNE 1997

Mike Tyson ensured his place in history as one of the most notorious boxers ever when he was disqualified for twice biting WBA heavyweight champion Evander Holyfield's ears. Both Americans were on a $35million guarantee for the rematch after Tyson had been stopped seven months earlier. Tyson was the slight favourite and began well, but he grew frustrated in his belief that Holyfield was being allowed to head-butt him. Taking matters into his own hands, Tyson bit Holyfield's ear during a clinch in the third round. Referee Mills Lane penalised Tyson but allowed the fight to continue until Tyson bit the other ear, this time chewing a chunk off and leaving Lane with no option but to disqualify him. As with so many Tyson fights, the aftermath was chaotic and he took a swing at a police officer. He was later banned for 18 months for his part in what has become known as 'Bite Night'. It seemed there was no way back for Tyson – but his career was not over yet.

29th JUNE 2013

Matthew Macklin was left gasping for air, his face a picture of pain and shock, after being chopped down by the deadly accurate fists of Gennady Golovkin. The British challenger became the 24th knockout victim in 27 fights for the crowd-pleasing world middleweight champion who was obliterating everything put in front of him. The ruthless Kazakh assassin left Macklin writhing in agony on the canvas with a sickening left hand to the body in the third round. "I knew it would be an easy fight," said Golovkin.

30th JUNE 1975

Joe Bugner held Muhammad Ali to points for the second time in his career after going 15 rounds with the world heavyweight champion in the searing heat of Kuala Lumpur. But European champion Bugner, who also drew with Ali over 12 rounds in Las Vegas in 1973, was criticised for an over-cautious performance after Ali comfortably won on points. Born in Hungary in 1950, Bugner moved to Britain with his family in 1957 and beat the popular Henry Cooper aged just 21. That win did not endear Bugner to the British public and he later moved to Australia.

BOXING
On This Day
History, Facts & Figures
from Every Day of the Year

July

1st JULY 1987

Terry Marsh, known as the Fighting Fireman, seemed on the brink of big things after a successful first defence of his IBF world light-welterweight title against Japan's Akio Kameda at the Royal Albert Hall in London. But a couple of months after his seventh round win over Kameda, unbeaten Marsh announced he was surprisingly retiring aged 29. Marsh, from Essex, revealed he was suffering from epilepsy and could not box on.

2nd JULY 1921

Jack Dempsey, a former homeless hobo who travelled under freight trains at night, was a huge star in the 1920s and his fourth round world heavyweight title win over Frenchman Georges Carpentier was the first million dollar gate in boxing history. Promoter Tex Rickard had a purpose-built stadium – Boyle's Thirty Acres – put up in nine weeks in Jersey City where an official crowd of 80,183 generated $1,789,238 in gate receipts. It was also the first fight to be broadcast live on radio. Carpentier was a popular First World War hero but Dempsey received some bad press in the build-up for avoiding the draft. Angered by the crowd cheering the Frenchman, Dempsey twice floored Carpentier before knocking him out in the fourth round. Carpentier, who broke his thumb in the second round, returned to light-heavyweight to continue as world champion. Dempsey, who took the name Jack after the middleweight boxer Jack 'Nonpareil' Dempsey, learned to box in saloons for food and when he arrived in New York in 1916, his entire life belongings were in a paper bag. Five years later, Dempsey got $300,000 for fighting Carpentier (who got $200,000) and his fistic fame made him as big a star as the baseball player Babe Ruth. Dempsey later served in the Coast Guards during the Second World War.

3rd JULY 1933

Panama Al Brown successfully defended his world bantamweight title with a 15 round points decision over local hero Johnny King in Manchester. Brown, who was nearly six feet, was tall for a bantamweight and travelled the world as champion. Brown, whose real name was Alfonso Teofilo Brown, fought 15 times in Britain, losing only once by disqualification to Johnny Cuthbert.

JACK DEMPSEY, WORLD HEAVYWEIGHT CHAMPION, 1919-1926

4th JULY 1919

Jack Dempsey burst on to the scene with an astonishing annihilation of giant Jess Willard, who was five inches taller and 58 pounds heavier. Despite his physical advantages, Willard surrendered on his stool at the end of three rounds. Dempsey, 24, was a figure of frenzied, perpetual motion, making it impossible for Willard, 37, to catch him with his long jab. The Manassa Mauler broke Willard's jaw with a left hook in the first round, during which the champion was floored seven times. Dempsey thought the fight had finished and had to scramble back into the ring for the second round.

4th JULY 1912

American Ad Wolgast and Mexican Joe Rivers contrived to produce a rare occurrence when they both landed simultaneous blows to knock each other out in the 13th round. Weary Wolgast landed a haymaker to the chin, while Rivers delivered a body shot. Referee Jack Welch counted to ten, with neither rising but awarded the fight to Wolgast, who had landed on top of Rivers, as he claimed Wolgast had started to rise as he finished his count and had fallen last. But contemporary newspaper reports state that Welch, who had been selected by Wolgast, helped the champion to his feet.

5th JULY 1910

America was recovering from the repercussions of the first 'Fight of the Century' between Jack Johnson and James J Jeffries the previous day. Johnson's victory over Jeffries precipitated race riots across the country on the night of 4th July and continued throughout the next day. "At least 11 and perhaps as many as 26 people would die before it was over," Geoffrey C. Ward wrote in *Unforgivable Blackness*. It had not merely been a world heavyweight title fight; for some it was a battle between black and white. In a racially-tense atmosphere, Johnson – the first black heavyweight champion – dominated and knocked out the former undefeated champion, who had ended a five-year retirement, in the 15th round in Reno, Nevada.

6th JULY 1922

World super-featherweight champion Johnny Dundee earned a 15-round unanimous decision over Jackie Sharkey in Ebbet's Field,

Brooklyn. Dundee, who was born in Sicily but raised in the Hell's Kitchen ghetto of New York, won every round and dropped Sharkey in rounds four and five of his first title defence. Later, he would win the world featherweight title.

7th JULY 2007

Ukrainian Wladimir Klitschko gained revenge over Lamon Brewster when the American's corner pulled him out of the world heavyweight title fight before the seventh round in Cologne, Germany. Brewster had not fought for 15 months and in that time had eye surgery for a detached retina. When this book was published, 39-year-old Klitschko was still world heavyweight No 1 and Brewster was still the last person to have beaten him by fifth round stoppage for the WBO version of the world title in 2004. "I have waited for this fight for three years," Klitschko said, after the third defence of his IBF belt. "He took quite a beating." After losing to Brewster, Klitschko adopted a safety-first approach, utilising his height and reach behind single, long jabs. It was efficient rather than entertaining and was not to everyone's taste, but Klitschko would argue his fans in Germany – where he was based – and Ukraine did not complain.

8th JULY 1989

Ugandan-born London-based John Mugabi was crowned WBC light-middleweight champion after Frenchman Rene Jacquot twisted an ankle in the opening two minutes. Jacquot was knocked to the canvas by a glancing right and en route to the floor injured his left ankle. When he got to his feet, Jacquot could not put any weight on his left foot and was swiftly returned to the canvas before the referee stopped the fight. Jacquot, who had been France's first world champion in 30 years, cried on his stool after the frustrating end to his brief reign. Mugabi had won an Olympic silver medal at the 1980 Moscow Games before manager Mickey Duff convinced him to base himself in London for his professional career.

9th JULY 1974

Popular knockout specialist and former world bantamweight king Ruben Olivarez left Japan's Zensuke Utagawa unconscious for three minutes with a left uppercut and right hand in the seventh round.

The Mexican, who had floored Utagawa twice before the stoppage in an utterly dominant display, walked away with the WBC world featherweight title.

10th JULY 1951

Randolph Turpin pulled off the best ever win by a British boxer when he captured the world middleweight crown off Sugar Ray Robinson in front of 18,000 at Earls Court. Robinson met the unheralded Turpin, from Leamington Spa, at the end of an exhausting European tour and over a third of Britain tuned in to listen to the fight live on radio. Robinson was boxing's biggest star and few outside of Turpin's team believed he could pull off the upset. But the fight did not go as expected as Turpin tied up the champion and made Robinson miss. Robinson was bullied at close quarters by the stronger challenger and never found his rhythm. Turpin, meanwhile, was dominating with his unorthodox style of lunging in with his punches. Robinson looked resigned to defeat when Turpin, who travelled to the west London venue unnoticed by tube, was awarded a well-earned 15-round decision to leave the crowd singing 'For He's a Jolly Good Fellow'. "I found Robinson relatively easy to hit and there was nothing like the power in the punches that I expected," said Turpin, who earned £12,000 for humbling the best boxer in history in a huge upset. It remains the most glorious night in British boxing but Turpin did not have long to enjoy his success before preparing for a rematch across the Atlantic just 64 days later.

11th JULY 1961

Terry Downes was crowned world middleweight champion with a puzzling win over American Paul Pender at Wembley. Pender, cut above both eyes, surprisingly surrendered exhausted on his stool after nine rounds with his corner complaining he had been feeling ill. Downes became the first Briton to hold the world middleweight title since Randy Turpin after beating Pender, who he had lost to six months earlier and would lose to again in 1962.

12th JULY 1986

In one of the last great 15-round fights, Evander Holyfield captured his first world title with a split decision over Dwight Muhammad

RANDY TURPIN (RIGHT) ON THE FRONT FOOT AGAINST SUGAR RAY ROBINSON IN 1951

Qawi. Holyfield, Olympic bronze medallist two years earlier, earned the WBA cruiserweight belt after dominating the last five rounds. "Maybe I'm getting too old for this and will look for something else to do," Qawi said after. There was a rematch a year later and 12 more years of fighting for Qawi.

13th JULY 1980

Matthew Saad Muhammad lived up to his ring moniker of 'Miracle' by surviving a torrid eighth round to stop Alvaro Lopez in the 14th round. The American, who had beaten Lopez in 11 rounds two years previously, was rocking in the eighth round after being subjected to a pummelling of more than 20 unanswered punches. But Saad Muhammad, who was called 'Miracle' after being abandoned on the steps of a convent in Philadelphia as a young boy, repeatedly survived beatings to prevail through his career, as was the case in the rematch with Mexican Lopez. The eighth round assault had left Lopez empty and he never won another round as Saad Muhammad took control and forced the stoppage in the 14th after four knockdowns. A year later, after eight defences of the WBC world light-heavyweight title, Saad Muhammad's reign was over. Lopez had five world title challenges in total, none successful.

14th JULY 2002

The British Boxing Board of Control tried to ban it, so instead the Luxembourg Boxing Federation sanctioned David Haye-Dereck Chisora at Upton Park in east London. The British boxing authority banned both London heavyweights for their brawl at a post-fight press conference in Munich earlier in the year. But that did not prevent promoter Frank Warren staging the event via the authority of a foreign governing body. Within 48 hours of tickets going on sale, 20,000 had been snapped up. Amid the rain in front of 31,000 and with neither boxer holding a British boxing licence, Haye settled his festering feud with Chisora by twice leaving his rival slumped on the canvas from left hooks in a fifth round demolition. After the brawl, the ban, the distasteful trash-talk and the bout Haye and Chisora embraced in the ring. "After sharing the ring with Dereck I have a new-found respect for him. I didn't think he was that good," said Haye.

15th JULY 1931

Classy Cuban Kid Chocolate was at the peak of his powers when he stopped Benny Bass for the world super-featherweight title. Chocolate subdued the Kiev-born American slugger with his slick moves to force a seventh round stoppage. Chocolate, whose real name was Eligio Sardinias, arrived in America in 1928 and this win was the start of a series of big fights for him.

16th JULY 1947

Rocky Graziano gained revenge over Tony Zale with a sickening sixth round stoppage in the second of their three exciting encounters. It was Graziano's only win in their thrilling trilogy, one of the most famous in boxing history. Zale's head was hanging out of the ropes with Graziano pummelling it when the referee stopped the savage slugfest. Every time these two American immigrants met they produced a ferocious fight. After winning back the world middleweight title, Graziano took the ring microphone and said: "Hey mum, your bad boy done good. Somebody up there likes me." Graziano liked a wild lifestyle, drinking with the likes of Jake LaMotta, and was given a dishonorable discharge from the US Army for going absent without leave.

17th JULY 1907

Jack Johnson did not waste time in disposing of former world heavyweight champion Bob Fitzsimmons with a second round knockout win. At 44, Fitzsimmons had seen better days and was not helped by torn ligaments in his right elbow. However, Fitzsimmons had still only lost the world light-heavyweight title 19 months before the Cornishman took on Johnson in a non-title bout. It was an easy win and a good name on the record for Johnson, 29, who was over a year away from fighting for the world heavyweight title.

18th JULY 1932

Jack 'Kid' Berg – known as The Whitechapel Whirlwind – was one of Britain's most successful boxers in America and his last big fight there ended on a happy note when he got a split decision over Kid Chocolate at Madison Square Garden Bowl in New York. The former world light-welterweight champion, who fought an incredible 74 times in the States, came on strong in the latter stages of the 15-round non-title bout. Londoner Berg, who had inflicted Chocolate's first ever defeat in 1930, never fought for a world title again but a month after their rematch Chocolate was world super-featherweight champion.

19th JULY 1986

After a promising start, Frank Bruno disintegrated from the sixth round of his first world title attempt against 'Terrible' Tim Witherspoon, from Philadelphia. Making the most of a five-inch reach advantage in the WBA heavyweight title fight, the Londoner employed his jab to good use in the first five rounds but his stamina let him down and Witherspoon capitalised on the openings. A crowd of 40,000 at Wembley fell silent as Bruno, 24, was left stunned, still and slumped on the ropes under Witherspoon's attack of right-handers in the 11th round which prompted Terry Lawless to throw in the towel.

20th JULY 2002

Sugar Shane Mosley could never figure out fellow American Vernon Forrest, who beat him for a third time unanimously on points in defence of his WBC welterweight title in Indianapolis. Forrest had beaten Mosley six months earlier and also when they were amateurs in the 1992 Olympic trials and this disappointing encounter – dubbed 'Rematch of the Century' – never lived up to the hype with more clinching than punching. Forrest earned $3.42million in the best year of his career.

21st JULY 1927

Jack Dempsey took advantage of Jack Sharkey's decision to stop and talk to the referee in the seventh round by knocking out his unsuspecting opponent. "What was I supposed to do, write him a letter?" said Dempsey, who finished the fight early in the seventh round in front of 82,000 at Yankee Stadium. Sharkey had been fancied to win the fight for the right to fight Gene Tunney for the world heavyweight title. Sharkey was winning the eliminator when early in the seventh Dempsey landed a flurry of low blows. When Sharkey turned to the referee to complain, Dempsey clocked him with a left hook.

21st JULY 1982

Mexican great Salvador Sanchez was last seen in a boxing ring turning on the style in the second half of the fight before stopping Azumah Nelson in the 15th and final round. It was the ninth defence of his WBC featherweight title. Twenty-two days later, 23-year-old Sanchez was killed in a motorbike accident.

22nd JULY 1963

Just ten months after he had lost his world heavyweight title in 126 seconds, Floyd Patterson dared to face scowling Sonny Liston again. This time around in Las Vegas, Patterson lasted four seconds longer in another massacre. Patterson hid his face behind his peek-a-boo cupping arms, but it was no good and the fight was stopped after a left uppercut put him down for a third time. "I feel disgraced and ashamed," said Patterson. He added: "I felt good – until I got hit." Patterson's trainer Cus D'Amato said: "It was the same as last time, he didn't move around. We would have said something in the corner in between rounds but the guy knocked him out before we had a chance." In the ring afterwards, contender Cassius Clay challenged Liston to a fight, yelling: "Liston's not great, he'll fall in eight." Asked how long it will take him to beat Clay, Liston said: "One and a half rounds to catch him, and half a round to knock him out."

23rd JULY 1988

Tony Lopez recovered from an eighth round knockdown to pull off a shock unanimous points win over Rocky Lockridge for the IBF world super-featherweight title. Lopez was left flat on his back by a right in the eighth but then won the last four rounds, having particular success with left uppercuts, to take the title in a bloody battle that left Lockridge needing more than 40 stitches. Lopez won a rematch, also on points, a year later and then a world title at lightweight but two-time champion Lockridge was finished at the top after their encounters and later in life was homeless.

24th JULY 2004

Arturo Gatti stopped Leonard Dorin with a left hook to the body in the second round of a first defence of the WBC light-welterweight title in Atlantic City. "It feels good that I didn't have to go to the hospital after the fight for a change," said crowd-pleaser Gatti, the Italian-born Canadian who was involved in exciting encounters with Micky Ward, Ivan Robinson, Wilson Rodriguez, Angel Manfredy and Oscar De La Hoya. Romania-born Canada-based Dorin, a two-time Olympic bronze medallist, never fought again after suffering his first professional defeat.

25th JULY 1965

Freddie Mills, Britain's biggest boxing star during the Second World War and just after it, was found with a hole in his head and a gun nearby in his car at the back of his nightclub in Charing Cross Road. The former world light-heavyweight champion was 46 at the time and the inquest declared it was suicide. However, some have tried to connect his death to the Krays, Reggie and Ronnie, the gangster twins who controlled the underworld in London at the time. Other rumours and theories claim Mills was bisexual and killed himself as he feared the truth about his sexuality was about to be revealed.

25th JULY 2009

There were no doubts surrounding the circumstances of Vernon Forrest's death. The former world welterweight champion was victim of a drive-by shooting after he pulled up at a gas station in Atlanta. Three men tried to rob Forrest, who gave chase before walking back to his car and being shot several times.

26th JULY 1981

Mexican Lupe Pintor was growing in confidence when he controversially stopped Jovito Rengifo in the eighth round. The Venezuelan challenger complained the stoppage was premature after being felled by a left jab. Two judges had Rengifo leading against WBC bantamweight champion Pintor, who was making a sixth defence of his title.

26th JULY 2014

Gennady Golovkin took three rounds to demolish Australia's former world champion Daniel Geale amid a blur of punches at Madison Square Garden. Geale became the Kazakh's 27th KO from 30 fights in his 11th WBA world middleweight title defence in what was supposed to be the toughest fight of his career. Golovkin was born in Karaganda, then part of the old Soviet Union and now in Kazakhstan, to a Russian father, who was a coal miner, and a Korean mother. Two of his elder brothers were killed while serving in the Russian Army during his childhood and after beginning his career in Germany, he based himself in America.

27th JULY 1918

Two years before he would fight for the world title, Jack Dempsey hinted at his potential by chopping down 6ft 6in giant Fred Fulton in 18 seconds. Fulton had been due to challenge Jess Willard for the world heavyweight title earlier in the month but the fight was scrapped because the public opposed it happening during the First World War.

28th JULY 1990

He may have been closer to 40 rather than the 36 years of age in reports at the time but Dennis Andries overwhelmed the champion Jeff Harding – at least 11 years younger – to regain the WBC light-heavyweight title in Melbourne, Australia. Harding had stopped Andries in the 12th round a year previous to their rematch and was ahead on the scorecards at the halfway point with the British boxer looking spent. But the Londoner launched a furious assault in the seventh and Harding could not beat the count. Andries did a celebratory cartwheel but after two defences lost the title back to Harding on points, this time on the other side of the world in London.

29th JULY 2000

Kostya Tszyu comfortably dealt with an ageing Julio Cesar Chavez, the former three-weight world champion who lasted six rounds with the in-form Australia-based Russian in Arizona. "It looks like it's time for me to retire," said 38-year-old Chavez after being stopped by the WBC light-welterweight champion. Mexican Chavez was dropped for only the second time in his career by a right hand and when he got off his hands and knees he took more punishment until the referee stopped it. Despite his vow to retire, Chavez fought five more times in as many years.

BOXING
On This Day

History, Facts & Figures
from Every Day of the Year

August

30th JULY 1977

Carlos Monzon fought for the last time, ending his seven-year reign as world middleweight champion after 14 defences aged 34. Monzon hung up his gloves after realising he was in decline following the second of two close points wins over Colombian Rodrigo Valdez in Monte Carlo. "After the bout I looked in the mirror and said to myself Monzon was never floored, Monzon is a great champion, he must always be remembered as a great champion, so I quit," Monzon humbly said of himself. Monzon had been a fighting machine and one of the best middleweight champions of all time, but he found life after boxing harder to master and was later jailed for murder before dying in a car crash aged 52.

30th JULY 2004

It was Danny Williams's inconsistency that got him the call-up to be Mike Tyson's latest comeback opponent. The Brixton boxer had lost his British heavyweight title to Michael Sprott on points earlier in the year and, it was thought, would be an accommodating opponent for former world champion Tyson in Louisville. But Williams absorbed Tyson's early onslaught and late in the fourth launched a non-stop attack himself that left the bemused American crashing through the ropes and counted out. Tyson, 38, would box just once more. Williams got a world title shot later in the year, when Vitali Klitschko bounced him off the canvas like a rubber ball.

31st JULY 1916

Jimmy Wilde knocked out fellow Briton Johnny Hughes in the tenth round to defend his world flyweight title. The Welshman, who claimed to have 864 fights, was working as a PT instructor for the British Army at the Aldershot base at the time during the First World War.

1st AUGUST 1987

Mike Tyson had an early scare when he was staggered by a left uppercut from Tony Tucker, but went on to win on points to add the IBF title to his WBA and WBC belts. The American, just 21, became the first heavyweight to unify all three world title belts and later promoter Don King put a bejewelled crown and an ermine robe on him in a bizarre mock coronation. "I feel silly," said an embarrassed Tyson holding a spectre during the ceremony. "I think I destroyed his image of indestructibility," said Tucker after taking Tyson the distance and doing a cheeky Ali shuffle late on. Despite the win, Tyson was already getting into trouble and during training for Tucker in June, he was arrested for assaulting a car park attendant and later revealed he had to be talked out of retiring before the fight. On the same day in 2003, Tyson filed for bankruptcy, $38 million in debt.

2nd AUGUST 1980

Teofilo Stevenson beat the Soviet Union's Pyotr Zaev for his third consecutive Olympic heavyweight gold medal in Moscow. Professional boxing was banned in Cuba and Stevenson turned down a $5million offer to fight Muhammad Ali. He said: "I don't believe in professionalism, only in revolution. I tell these men from America, the promoters, that money means nothing to me. What is a million dollars against eight million Cubans who love me?" Stevenson's lethal right hand, footwork and ringcraft ensured a 4-1 win over Zaev and he might have won a fourth gold had Cuba not boycotted the 1984 Olympics. Stevenson won 302 and lost 22 of his amateur bouts.

3rd AUGUST 1912

Six months after losing his world featherweight title, Abe Attell was held to a 20-round draw with Harlem Tommy Murphy in what was a bloodbath in Daly City, California. The rematch, after Murphy had beaten Attell earlier in the year, was scored a draw after they finished so covered in blood it was hard to tell them apart. One report at the time said the pair were "covered in gore from head to knee."

4th AUGUST 2007

The chemistry that was created when Mexicans Israel Vazquez and Rafael Marquez shared a ring demanded they fought four times in three years. Each bout was entertaining, non-stop action and Vazquez levelled their series in the second encounter to win back the WBC super-bantamweight title after a stunning shootout in the border town of Hidalgo in Texas. The pair went toe-to-toe in an incredible third round that saw Marquez wobbled by a left hook and both were cut around the eyes. Vazquez, who was stopped due to a nose injury in the first fight, dropped Marquez in the sixth with a right uppercut followed by a left hook and then finished him off when he got back up. Vazquez won a points decision a year later but was then stopped by Marquez – younger brother of Juan Manuel – in the third round of their fourth fight. The series ended 2-2 and took its toll: Vazquez never boxed again and Marquez was never the same fighter.

5th AUGUST 2006

Edwin Valero was taken into unknown territory – beyond the second round – for the first time in his career when he challenged Panamanian Vicente Mosquera for the WBA super-featherweight title in Panama City. Eighteen of Valero's first 19 bouts had ended in the first round and Mosquera looked to be heading the same way when he was floored twice in the first three minutes. But the champion survived to send Valero to the canvas for the first time in his career in the third round. Valero was in a real scrap for once but from the sixth he began to take control before forcing a tenth round stoppage.

6th AUGUST 1993

Gerald McClellan forged a frightening reputation for himself in the middleweight division with performances like his devastating 20-second knockout of Jay Bell in his first WBC world title defence. The wicked, left body shot left Bell crumpled in a heap for the quickest KO in world title history. Puerto Rican Daniel Jimenez broke McClellan's record a year later with a 17-second KO of Austrian Harald Geier for the WBO super-bantamweight belt. McClellan's win over his fellow American Bell in Puerto Rico remains the second fastest KO in world title fight history.

7th AUGUST 1997

Roy Jones Jr took just two minutes and 31 seconds to get revenge for his first ever defeat and regain the WBC light-heavyweight title. Five months earlier, Montell Griffin had been handed victory after Jones, who at the time was a three-division world champion, was disqualified for hitting his opponent while he was down.

8th AUGUST 1966

Nine days after Bobby Moore had lifted the World Cup for England at Wembley, London hosted another global sporting event when Muhammad Ali visited to defend his world heavyweight title. This time, there was no glory in the outcome as Brian London, known as The Blackpool Rock, obligingly crumbled in three rounds to the visiting American. London had suffered three defeats to British champion Henry Cooper by the time he faced Ali and seven years after Floyd Patterson stopped London in a previous world title challenge. Ali's previous defence had also been in London against Cooper, who was stopped on a cut in the sixth round. Back in London to face London, Ali took just three rounds to earn $252,000, as well as television money.

8th AUGUST 1992

Cuba dominated the Barcelona Olympics, with Felix Savon and Joel Casamayor among the seven gold medallists. Casamayor beat Wayne McCullough in the 54kg category in a clash of two future world champions while McCullough's Irish team-mate Michael Carruth won gold at 67kg. Star of the tournament was American Oscar De La Hoya, who became known as the Golden Boy after winning the 60kg gold against German Marco Rudolph.

9th AUGUST 2012

Nicola Adams, Katie Taylor and Claressa Shields won golds in the first ever women's Olympic boxing tournament at London 2012. Great Britain's Adams sent her home crowd wild as she outclassed China's Ren Cancan to win 16-7 in the flyweight final. Lightweight Taylor, who looked good enough to beat some of the men in the Olympic tournament, won Ireland's first gold medal since 1996 after coming from behind in the last round to beat Russia's Sofya

Ochigava 10-8 on points. Middleweight Shields was America's only boxing medallist at 2012 after she outpointed Russian Nadezda Torlopova 19-12.

10th AUGUST 2014

Some of the most famous moments in boxing have been shocks, but has there been anything so astonishing as the morning when promoter Frank Maloney revealed (through a Sunday tabloid) that he was now a woman? Maloney, who managed Lennox Lewis among others, declared he was undergoing a sex change, was having corrective treatment and should now be known as Kellie. He claimed he had known he was a woman in a man's body since the age of four. It seemed incredulous since Maloney had excelled in the macho boxing business due to his pugnacious manner that prompted American rival Don King to once call him "a mental midget". People who had known Maloney for decades, even his own brother Eugene, were left astounded. Maloney had recently finished his 30-year career as a promoter and manager and in recent years had also suffered a heart attack, tried to commit suicide, discovered boxer Darren Sutherland hanged and split from his second wife. In the week following the sex-change revelation, the 61-year-old father of three entered the reality TV show *Celebrity Big Brother* (for a reported £400,000 fee).

11th AUGUST 1984

There was a gold rush for America in the 1984 Olympic finals day. The hosts bagged nine gold medals – Paul Gonzales, Steve McCrory, Meldrick Taylor, Pernell Whitaker, Jerry Page, Mark Breland, Frank Tate, Henry Tillman and Tyrell Biggs – as well as one silver from Virgil Hill. One American boxer who missed out on the fun was Evander Holyfield, who had to settle for bronze in the 81kg class but would go on to become more successful than any of his team-mates in the professional ranks.

12th AUGUST 1959

Yvon Durelle, the Canadian known as The Fighting Fisherman, was not in the right frame of mind when he lost a rematch to Archie Moore for the world light-heavyweight title. Durelle was still in mourning at the loss of friends and relatives who were among the 35 people from his home village by the sea to have been killed by a tidal wave two months previously. Durelle was knocked down four times in a three round loss, but their first fight had been closer with Moore winning in the 11th round after being floored three times in the first round.

13th AUGUST 1994

Riddick Bowe escaped being disqualified after he knocked out Buster Mathis Jr with a right while he was down on one knee during the fourth round of a non-title fight. Bowe's first fight since he lost the world heavyweight title nine months previously was ruled a no-contest. "You were down, I didn't know, I'm sorry," Bowe said to Mathis.

14th AUGUST 1903

James J Corbett's cornerman threw a palm leaf into the ring to alert the referee to stop the world heavyweight title fight with James J Jeffries early in the tenth round at Mechanic's Pavilion in San Francisco. The aging Corbett, who had been world champion from 1892 to 1897 and hired a young Jeffries as a sparring partner before his fight with Bob Fitzsimmons, had taken enough punishment and had just been felled by a body shot at the time of the stoppage. It was enough to put off Corbett from fighting again as this was his second stoppage defeat to Jeffries. Corbett became an actor while Jeffries would make one more defence before retiring. Known as The Boilermaker, Jeffries then ended a six-year retirement in 1910 to take on Jack Johnson.

15th AUGUST 1966

Jose Torres made three defences of his WBA-WBC light-heavyweight title in 18 months and his second against Eddie Cotton was voted fight of the year. Torres, a Puerto Rican who had learned to box in the US Army, prevailed on a unanimous points decision after 15 brutal rounds in Las Vegas. "There's no doubt in my mind that I won the fight," said Cotton, 40, and many in the Las Vegas Convention Center agreed. "The only body shot he hurt me with was a foul," said Torres, 30, referring to a low blow that cost Cotton a point. New York-based Torres was a stylish boxer who also won an Olympic silver medal and after boxing wrote acclaimed books on Muhammad Ali and Mike Tyson as well as becoming a leading administrator of the sport. Cotton never got the rematch he called for or another title shot.

16th AUGUST 1743

English champion Jack Broughton was the first person to draw up a set of boxing rules from his boxing venue at Tottenham Court Road, London. Broughton published the rules for the bare-knuckle sport after one of his opponents George Stevenson died from injuries sustained in a fight with him two years previously.

17th AUGUST 1938

Henry Armstrong's split points decision over Lou Ambers for the world lightweight title made him the reigning champion at three weight divisions (featherweight, welterweight and lightweight). Armstrong's unprecedented feat was even more remarkable in that he won three of the eight world titles available within ten months at a time when the world title was not fractured by four belts in each division like it is today. Ambers came close in thwarting Armstrong's triple crown success in an intense scrap. Armstrong's mouth bled heavily from the third round and in the tenth round the referee was about to stop the fight because of all the blood on the canvas. "Don't stop it, I'll stop bleeding," Armstrong pleaded. Armstrong fought on without his mouthpiece and swallowed his blood for six rounds as his work-rate got him the verdict. Armstrong held the featherweight, lightweight and welterweight titles simultaneously for four months until he relinquished the featherweight belt, lost the lightweight strap to Ambers and went on defending the welterweight title for another two years.

18th AUGUST 1979

John Conteh seemed on the brink of regaining the WBC world light-heavyweight title in the 12th round against Matthew Saad Muhammad in Atlantic City. Conteh's precise jab and a half-blind Saad Muhammad left the Liverpool boxer in control going into the remaining three rounds. Conteh's astute trainer George Francis became suspicious about the methods used in the opposing corner and had complained after the ninth round about the solution used by Saad Muhammad's corner on a cut that stretched across the American's entire left eyebrow. But the protest was ignored, the bleeding was stemmed and Saad Muhammad went on to twice floor the British challenger in the 14th round and earn a unanimous points decision. But Francis was vindicated when tests on the swabs taken from the champion's corner found an illegal adrenalin chloride solution mixed with ground tea leaves was used to stop the bleeding.

19th AUGUST 1995

Mike Tyson's first fight after being released from serving three years in prison for rape was much hyped but short on action as it only lasted 89 seconds. Peter McNeeley was selected as the former champion's comeback opponent and after sprinting out of his corner swinging punches, he was comically on the floor within ten seconds from a Tyson right hook. McNeeley continued but when a right uppercut returned him to the canvas his manager Vinnie Vecchione entered the ring, leaving referee Mills Lane to disqualify McNeeley, who was consoled by a $540,000 pay day for less than two minutes' work. But McNeeley's income was nothing compared to Tyson's $25million. Tyson, 29, was back after four years out of the ring and within a year he was world heavyweight champion again.

20th AUGUST 1954

World middleweight champion Carl 'Bobo' Olson climbed off the canvas in the 11th round to defeat Rocky Castellani by a unanimous points decision. Olson almost lost the title on the scales when he weighed in eight ounces over but was allowed two hours to boil off the excess weight. But the Hawaiian boxer did not appear weight-drained in the fight, relentlessly marching forward. Olson got up at the count of three after tripping over Castellani's legs in the 11th round and landed a right to the jaw that almost had Castellani counted out in the 12th round. Castellani, who fractured a bone in his left hand, never fought for the title again.

21st AUGUST 1956

Peter Rademacher won heavyweight gold at the Melbourne Olympics with three knockout wins and such was the hype around him that a year and one day later he found himself in the ring challenging world heavyweight champion Floyd Patterson on his professional debut. It was a rude awakening to the punch-for-pay game as Rademacher was floored six times in a six-round defeat.

22nd AUGUST 1969

Mexican Ruben Olivares scooped up Lionel Rose and led him back to his corner after his five-round beating of the Aboriginal boxer for the world bantamweight title. The last round was painful for Rose, who had won the title only a year earlier. But his brief reign had given heart to Aborigines as he became a national hero in Australia. Olivares led the way at a rich time for bantamweights and would later step up to win a world title at featherweight.

22nd AUGUST 1998

It was referee Mills Lane who inflicted the injury that left Bernard Hopkins unable to continue in a world middleweight title defence. Throughout Hopkins's bout with fellow American Robert Allen, there had been a lot of holding and when Lane tried to free Hopkins from a head lock, he inadvertently shoved the champion through the ropes. Hopkins injured his right ankle in the fall and insisted he could not continue, with the fight declared a no-contest.

23rd AUGUST 1986

Julian Jackson went on to become a three-time and two-weight world champion but his first experience at the top level was a brief and painful one. Jackson was dispatched in the second round of an explosive bout with WBA light-middleweight champion Mike McCallum. Unbeaten Jamaican McCallum knocked down Jackson with a left and when the Virgin Islands boxer got up he moved in to finish him off. Afterwards, Jackson dedicated his life to God and was world champion a year later.

23rd AUGUST 2008

James DeGale won Britain's first Olympic gold medal since super-heavyweight Audley Harrison in 2000 when he outpointed Cuban Emilio Correa in the middleweight final. Ukrainian Vasyl Lomachenko was an impressive winner of the 57kg division, stopping Frenchman Khedafi Djelkhir in the first round.

24th AUGUST 2008

Zou Shiming won host nation China's first ever Olympic boxing gold medal after Mongolia's Serdamba Purevdorj was forced to retire with an injury 19 seconds into the second round of the light-flyweight final in Beijing. Shiming – China's most successful amateur boxer ever – won gold again four years later in London before turning professional.

25th AUGUST 1950

Sugar Ray Robinson needed just 52 seconds to knock out Jose Basora and win the Pennsylvania State version of the world middleweight title. Basora hit the deck four times before he was counted out after being caught cold by the early onslaught. Robinson had wanted to make a statement after being jeered by the crowd following a 15-round defence of his world welterweight title two weeks previously against Charley Fusari. The first round blow-out was a surprise: Puerto Rican Basora was one of only two men to avoid defeat to Robinson in the first eight years and 55 fights of his career, when he held the American maestro to a ten-round draw in 1945.

26th AUGUST 1995

Pernell Whitaker coasted to a unanimous points decision in defence of his WBC welterweight title against Scotsman Gary Jacobs in Atlantic City. The skilful American was given a count in the 11th round but TV replays showed it was a slip that put him down. Embarrassed, Whitaker cranked it up a notch in the last round to twice floor Jacobs in the final 30 seconds. Jacobs, who was on his back when the final bell went, was also docked a point for excessive holding in the last round, making the lopsided scores 117-109, 118-109 and 118-107.

27th AUGUST 1943

Jack Dempsey, the former world heavyweight champion, once said of Henry Armstrong: "He was a human piston. I never saw a better small man and I never expect to." But by now the little buzz-saw had run flat and Armstrong's relentless punching was not what it once was when he met contender Sugar Ray Robinson in front of 15,371 at Madison Square Garden. It was a collision of the former and future world welterweight champions – but it was far from competitive. Robinson, who at the time was a corporal in the US Army during the Second World War, won every round of a ten-round non-title fight. Armstrong announced his retirement immediately after the fight but returned to the ring a year later before finishing in 1945. Robinson, who was still three years away from getting a belated shot at the world title, was reported to have taken it easy on Armstrong in an utterly dominant display.

28th AUGUST 1959

Gene Fullmer stopped fellow former champion Carmen Basilio early in the 14th round for the world middleweight title, which had been stripped from Sugar Ray Robinson for inactivity. Fullmer regained the belt he lost to Robinson in 1957 but for Italian-American Basilio it was the first of three failed attempts to win back the belt. Basilio, a former onion picker from Canastota, was worn down in a slugging match and when he was taking hard rights pressed against the ropes in the 14th, his trainer Angelo Dundee called for it to be stopped. This fight was so good the pair met again a year later, when Fullmer got the job done two rounds quicker. Fullmer, a Mormon from Utah, would reign for three years.

29th AUGUST 2004

Amir Khan, a 17-year-old from Bolton, had to settle for silver after a plucky run to the Olympic lightweight final, where he was out-pointed by Cuban Mario Kindelan. Cuba again dominated with Guillermo Rigondeaux, Yuriolkis Gamboa, Yan Barthelemi and Odlanier Solis all winning golds in Athens. Russian Alexander Povetkin and American Andre Ward also won gold but Kazakhstan's Gennady Golovkin had to settle for silver.

29th AUGUST 1960

The real drama did not start until Dick Richardson had retained his European heavyweight title after British rival Brian London was pulled out by his corner at the end of the eighth round due to a bad cut. London, known as The Blackpool Rock, was upset because he felt the cut was caused by a head-butt in the seventh round of a bad-tempered bout. With the ring announcer about to go through the formalities, London piled into Richardson's trainer Johnny Lewis which sparked a brawl in the ring between the fighters' cornermen, managers and family. Police flooded the ring to break it up in what

BOXING
On This Day
History, Facts & Figures
from Every Day of the Year

September

became known as the 'Brawl in Porthcawl'. "When it was finished I went over to shake hands with Richardson and some little fellow took a swing at me," said London. "So I had a go back."

30th AUGUST 1937

Nobody expected Welshman Tommy Farr to extend Joe Louis the full 15-round distance in the champion's first defence of the world heavyweight title. But by the end, most of the 36,903 crowd at New York's Yankee Stadium were booing the unanimous decision for Louis in what was the first of a record 25 defences. Farr, a Welsh miner, earned his best ever pay day ($60,000) for a gallant effort and was one of only two men to go the 15-round distance with Louis. After a four-day delay to the fight being staged, due to poor ticket sales and the weather, two million people in Britain tuned in to the radio during the early hours of the morning. Farr kept bouncing back from Louis's beautifully delivered combinations and, with cuts under his eyes, won some of the later rounds. When news of the fight reached Farr's home village of Tonypandy at 4am, people in the streets began singing 'Land of our Fathers'. Farr said years later: "Every time I hear the name Joe Louis my nose starts to bleed."

31st AUGUST 1918

Welshman Jimmy Wilde, regarded by historians as the best flyweight ever, received a purse of diamonds for his 12th round stoppage of English rival Joe Conn at Stamford Bridge. Since he was a company sergeant major based at Aldershot in the final months of the First World War, Wilde could not receive any money for the bout. So, instead, he received diamonds worth £2,000. After the American Peter Herman, who he would meet in 1921, Wilde considered Conn his best opponent, but Wilde put him down 13 times before the referee stopped it. "I had a bit of a tussle for the first three or four rounds but in the last four rounds there was only one in it," said Wilde. Wilde looked like one of the figures in a Lowry painting with his matchstick limbs, but he is arguably the greatest British boxer of all time. Known as The Mighty Atom, 5ft 2in Wilde was unorthodox, powerful and had impeccable timing. He was born in Merthyr Tydfil and began work as a pit boy aged 12. By 16 he had forged a reputation for himself in the boxing booths and claimed to have had 864 bouts, knocking out 675 opponents.

1st SEPTEMBER 1983

Kiko Bejines left the ring unconscious on a stretcher after being knocked out by a huge right hand from Alberto Davila in the last round of their vacant WBC world bantamweight title fight. Mexican Bejines, ahead on points, faded badly in the last round and three days later, following surgery to remove a blood clot from his brain, died in hospital. Bejines, 20, never regained consciousness and his wife was pregnant with their first child at the time of his death. His death led to more calls for boxing to be banned after the death the previous year of South Korea's Deuk-Koo Kim and of Welshman Johnny Owen in 1980.

2nd SEPTEMBER 1995

After failed world title attempts against Tim Witherspoon, Mike Tyson and Lennox Lewis, Frank Bruno fought off fatigue in the final round to beat American Oliver McCall on points for the WBA world heavyweight title at Wembley. Bruno made a fast start but slowed dramatically in the later rounds. McCall, who had pulled off a shock a year earlier by stopping Lewis, went for it in the last round but Bruno, roared on by 30,000 fans, held on for a unanimous decision. Bruno said: "That last round was very tough and he came at me like a madman. All I could do was try to survive and I did survive. I look like ET but I'm a winner, a champion." Promoter Frank Warren promised Bruno a Bentley as a winning bonus. "The first thing he said after winning the fight was, where's my Bentley?" said Warren.

3rd SEPTEMBER 1906

Joe Gans entered the ring so dangerously weight-drained for his world lightweight title fight with Battling Nelson that afterwards he came down with tuberculosis. Nelson's manager Billy Nolan insisted that Gans could not replenish his body properly after the weigh-in and the American was further hampered when he broke his hand in the 33rd round. But the speed and skill of Gans, an early pioneer for black boxers, saw him frustrate the Danish boxer until Nelson was penalised for yet another low blow and disqualified in the 42nd round in Goldfield, Nevada.

4th SEPTEMBER 1982

After Kirkland Laing pulled off the biggest global upset of the year with a split decision over Roberto Duran in Detroit, the former British welterweight champion vanished. After months partying, Laing resurfaced a year later but by then the momentum was lost. Laing never fulfilled his potential due to his indulgence in alcohol and drugs. "I had too much early and wasn't man enough or mature enough to handle it," said Laing. In the next two years after losing to Laing, Duran would earn millions in world title fights against Davey Moore, Marvin Hagler and Thomas Hearns. Laing never earned much nor fought for a world title.

5th SEPTEMBER 1960

The 16,000 in attendance at the Palazzo dello Sport in Rome did not know it at the time, but they were witnessing the birth of sport's biggest ever star when an unknown American 18-year-old called Cassius Clay won Olympic light-heavyweight gold. The Louisville boxer beat Zbigniew Pietrzykowski but Clay, who later renamed himself Muhammad Ali, nearly did not travel to Italy because of a fear of flying. He even brought his own parachute for the flight over. Clay battered the Pole in the last round to earn the points decision.

6th SEPTEMBER 2014

Northern Ireland's biggest ever boxing crowd – 16,000 – turned out at a purpose built stadium on the slipway where the *Titanic* was built just over 100 years earlier to see local hero Carl Frampton win the IBF super-bantamweight title. Frampton had already beaten Kiko Martinez 18 months previously, but it was the Spaniard who went on to win a version of the world title. When they met again on a chilly night, unbeaten Frampton did not freeze on the biggest night of his life and decked Martinez in round five en route to a unanimous decision. Victory also confirmed Frampton's status as Northern Ireland's most popular boxer since Barry McGuigan reigned as world featherweight champion (1985-86). McGuigan was promoter of the show and said: "I've been telling everyone for years he would be world champion. This kid could end up being the best Irish fighter who ever lived."

7th SEPTEMBER 1892

Boxing's modern era was ushered in with the first world heavyweight title bout under the Marquess of Queensberry Rules – three-minute rounds, ten-second count for a knockout and the use of boxing gloves – which saw bareknuckle champion John L Sullivan outboxed by James J Corbett, who won by KO in the 21st round at the Olympic Club in New Orleans. Sullivan, slower and fatter after enjoying his fame as world champion, was cut to shreds by the younger and more mobile challenger. Ex-bank clerk Corbett, from California, would reign for five years. World featherweight champion George Dixon and world lightweight champion Jack McAuliffe defended their belts on the same bumper bill called 'Carnival of Champions'.

8th SEPTEMBER 1950

Willie Pep was a masterful boxer and known as Will o' the Wisp because he was so elusive. However, Sandy Saddler was one opponent who got the better of him. Pep was controlling the fight, despite being knocked down for a count of nine in the third round, until he dislocated his shoulder in the seventh round and did not emerge for the eighth. Pep claimed he dislocated his left shoulder in a clinch because of Saddler's wrestling. Pep had regained the world featherweight title in February 1949 from Saddler, who had knocked him out four months previously. Pep and Saddler met for the fourth and final time on 26 September, 1951 in a foul-filled contest that Pep – ahead on the scorecards – quit after nine rounds with blood running into his eyes. Saddler won their series 3-1.

9th SEPTEMBER 1983

Alexis Arguello was foiled in his bid to become the first boxer to win a world title in a fourth weight division when he was knocked out for the second time in a year by WBA light-welterweight champion Aaron Pryor. Nicaraguan Arguello was down in the first, fourth and tenth rounds and was counted out sitting on the canvas in Las Vegas.

9th SEPTEMBER 1995

Chris Eubank failed in his attempt to win back the WBO world super-middleweight title from Irishman Steve Collins, who once again won on points in front of his home fans. Eubank announced his retirement after the bout – but returned for five more fights.

10th SEPTEMBER 1931

Tony Canzoneri knocked down Jack 'Kid' Berg twice as he defended his world lightweight and light-welterweight titles by unanimous decision, but the Briton was left feeling aggrieved about a low blow that went unpunished. The Italian-American legitimately floored Berg in the opening round at the Polo Grounds in New York and it looked like it would be another early night for him. Canzoneri had beaten Berg for both lightweight and light-welterweight titles in three rounds five months previously, but the Londoner rose at the count of nine. Berg hit the canvas again in the eighth round from a low left hook, but under the local rules a fighter could not win or lose on a foul so Berg had no choice but to get up at nine to continue.

11th SEPTEMBER 1925

World light-heavyweight champion Paul Berlenbach knocked out Jimmy Slattery in the 11th round at the Yankee Stadium. Ex-wrestler Berlenback, who had only been a professional boxer two years, forced three knockdowns in the 11th. New Yorker Berlenbach got $32,000 for his second of three defences after winning the belt off Mike McTigue earlier in 1925. Slattery, from Buffalo, went on to hold the world title briefly in 1927 and 1930 while Berlenbach made one more defence.

12th SEPTEMBER 1951

Just 64 days after the jubilant scenes at Earls Court following his triumph over Sugar Ray Robinson, Randolph Turpin's reign as world middleweight champion was ended by a punishing stoppage in the tenth round in front of 61,370 at the Polo Grounds in New York. The rematch was delicately poised when Turpin split Robinson's left eyebrow in the tenth and blood gushed from the wound like a spring. Fearing the referee was about to intervene, Robinson produced a blistering attack and dropped Turpin. The Briton got to his feet but was then pinned against the ropes and Robinson unloaded a frenzied assault, with some of the punches illegal. Robinson swarmed all over Turpin until a right, flush on the chin, prompted referee Ruby Goldstein to stop it with eight seconds of the tenth round left. The fight was even when it was stopped. Goldstein scored it four rounds apiece, with one even, up to the tenth round.

SUGAR RAY LEONARD AND TRAINER ANGELO DUNDEE (LEFT) DURING THE FIGHT AGAINST TOMMY HEARNS IN 1981

13th SEPTEMBER 1971

Fans of the film series Rocky starring Sylvester Stallone have Ken Buchanan to thank for one of its most memorable – and gory – moments. Stallone re-enacted a scene from Buchanan's WBA world lightweight title defence against Ismael Laguna in *Rocky* (1976). When Buchanan sat on his stool at the end of the third round with his left eye closed, his canny cornerman Eddie Thomas performed emergency surgery. Thomas quickly ran a razor blade over the swelling, producing a gush of blood and deflating the 'mouse'. Buchanan, who would later need ten stitches, could once again partially see out of his left eye and jabbed his way to a points win at Madison Square Garden.

14th SEPTEMBER 1923

It lasted just three minutes and 57 seconds, but there was more entertainment in that time than the entire careers of some recent world heavyweight champions. Jack Dempsey floored Luis Angel Firpo nine times and was knocked out of the ring himself before stopping the challenger in the second round of his last successful world heavyweight title defence, in front of a crowd of 85,800 at the Polo Grounds. Argentine Firpo had been down seven times before the Wild Bull of the Pampas charged at Dempsey, who was sent through the ropes on to a press table by a right to the temple. Dempsey, who landed on a typewriter, was then helped by Firpo's reticence to attack before delivering a right cross that left Firpo flat on his back and counted out.

15th SEPTEMBER 1978

Muhammad Ali was a shell of his former self but at 36 he still had enough ambition to jab and grab his way to a unanimous decision over Leon Spinks. The American won back the world heavyweight crown for an unprecedented third time and a year later announced he had retired; but there were still two more damaging fights left for Ali. Over 63,000 saw Ali's rematch with Spinks, 25, at the Superdome in New Orleans, after Spinks had won a points decision earlier in the year. Ali economically outboxed Spinks and repeatedly smothered him in bear hugs to secure victory. Spinks's life had spun out of control since beating Ali; he drank excessively and was arrested four times for driving offences and drug possession.

16th SEPTEMBER 1981

Sugar Ray Leonard was trailing on all three scorecards and needed a knockout when fading Thomas Hearns was stopped in the 14th round of their $35million world welterweight title unification fight. Hearns was winning in front of a global TV audience of 300 million and at the end of the 12th round when Leonard sat on his stool, his trainer Angelo Dundee said: "You're blowing it, son." It inspired a big round for Leonard, who floored Hearns in the final moments of the 13th. Hearns, who was ahead on points (125-122, 125-121, 124-122), was then sent through the ropes by a barrage of blows in the 14th to prompt the stoppage. "Tommy seemed like an indestructible machine, so to beat him was my defining moment," said Leonard.

17th SEPTEMBER 2011

Knockouts are scarce on Floyd Mayweather Jr's record late in his career and one of the rare such occasions when the American finished business early was when he sucker-punched Victor Ortiz in the fourth round. Ortiz forgot to adhere to the referee's pre-bout instructions: Protect yourself at all times. In the fourth round, Ortiz was deducted a point by referee Joe Cortez for a head butt. When the fight continued, Ortiz kept his hands at his side looking at Cortez after trying to hug Mayweather, who clocked him with a short left hook followed by a right.

18th SEPTEMBER 2004

Bernard Hopkins became the first boxer to knock out Oscar De La Hoya with a paralysing left hook to his liver in the ninth round. Hopkins, 39, called the shot "chopped liver with Hopkins sauce" that inflicted De La Hoya's first stoppage loss after 12 years as a professional. All four world middleweight title belts were on the line at the MGM Grand in Las Vegas, with the bigger and stronger Hopkins ahead on two of the three scorecards at the time of the stoppage. De La Hoya had two other big fights in Vegas on this date: forcing Mexican Julio Cesar Chavez to retire after eight rounds in 1998 and a year later losing on points to Puerto Rican Felix Trinidad after he eased off in the latter rounds believing he had won the world welterweight title unification fight.

19th SEPTEMBER 1980

Welshman Johnny Owen never regained consciousness after being knocked out by WBC bantamweight champion Lupe Pintor in Los Angeles. Owen, who was known as the Merthyr Matchstick due to his lanky frame, was too brave for his own good and refused to succumb until he was sickeningly separated from his senses in the 12th round. Owen bored in during the early rounds but by the fifth round the heavier-hitting Mexican had taken control. Owen was floored in the ninth and 12th rounds before being finally flattened by a ferocious right that left him unconscious before he hit the floor. After brain surgery to remove a blood clot, Owen could not be saved and died in November.

20th SEPTEMBER 1972

Floyd Patterson endured a painful night the last time he was seen in a boxing ring, when Muhammad Ali stopped him in seven rounds at Madison Square Garden. But it was not as bad as the previous time former world heavyweight champion Patterson had lost to Ali in a cruel 12-round beating in 1965. This time, 37-year-old Patterson was mercifully stopped after his left eye was swollen shut from Ali's stinging blows.

21st SEPTEMBER 1989

A 62-year-old mother took matters into her own hands when her son was taking a beating in a British light-heavyweight title eliminator. During the third round, Minna Wilson climbed into the ring to land the winning blow herself. Her son Tony was on the ropes when Mrs Wilson clobbered her son's opponent Steve McCarthy on the head with her high-heeled shoe. The fight was stopped and, incredibly, awarded to Wilson because McCarthy refused to carry on.

21st SEPTEMBER 1991

It had been a thrilling, epic encounter but all that was forgotten when Michael Watson collapsed in the ring following his final round defeat to Chris Eubank for the WBO world super-middleweight title at White Hart Lane. After being caught by a vicious right uppercut at the end of the 11th round, Watson's head whiplashed off the bottom rope on the way to the canvas. Watson got up and when he came out for the 12th round, he was met by 26 unanswered punches before the fight was stopped. Watson was left with brain damage but his fighting spirit saw him complete the London marathon in 2003.

22nd SEPTEMBER 1927

World heavyweight champion Gene Tunney was gifted vital seconds in 'The Battle of the Long Count' to get off the canvas and beat Jack Dempsey for a second time on points at Soldier's Field in Chicago. Referee Dave Barry delayed issuing a count that allowed Tunney longer refuge for his head to clear before getting up and regaining control of the ten-round bout. Tunney, who had won the title from Dempsey a year previously, was dropped in the seventh round and when Barry ordered Dempsey to retreat to a neutral corner, he delayed. Barry only started the count once Dempsey was in a neutral corner and Tunney sensibly got up at the count of nine – after 14 seconds had elapsed. Tunney then back-pedalled and got his jab working again in the eighth before he dropped Dempsey with a right to the jaw. After ten rounds the decision was Tunney's and a $1million cheque. Mobster Al Capone lost $45,000 betting on Dempsey after hearing that Tunney had been reading Shakespeare. More importantly, Capone was also banking on there being a different referee to Barry, who was appointed on the afternoon of the fight. The 104,943 crowd generated an income of $2,658,660.

23rd SEPTEMBER 1952

Rocky Marciano was sent to the canvas for the first time in his career by Jersey Joe Walcott – but got up to knock out his fellow American and win the world heavyweight title. A left hook early in the first round floored Marciano, but he was up at the count of four. Marciano was trailing on all three scorecards when he stopped Walcott with a short right hand in the 13th round. In a rematch the following year, Walcott was ironed out on the canvas in the first round.

24th SEPTEMBER 1994

On-off crack addict Oliver McCall walked to the ring crying as if on the verge of breakdown before facing Lennox Lewis. But it was the unstable American who left Wembley Arena with the WBC heavyweight title after capitalising on a lazy jab from Lewis with a right hook. Lewis collapsed to the canvas and when he got to his feet the referee waved the fight off 31 seconds into round two. Lewis would then hire McCall's trainer Emanuel Steward to begin his rehabilitation.

25th SEPTEMBER 1962

Floyd Patterson felt so ashamed of being obliterated in a round by Sonny Liston that the former world heavyweight champion sneaked out of Comiskey Park in Chicago in disguise, with a fake moustache and glasses, and drove through the night back to New York. The fact that Patterson travelled to the venue with a disguise told a lot about his belief in beating Liston. Patterson's speed and skills were no match for Liston's brute strength and he was stopped in 126 seconds.

26th SEPTEMBER 1970

Ken Buchanan suffered sunburn as he pulled off one of the best ever victories by a British boxer overseas with a split points win over Ismael Laguna to lift the WBA world lightweight title in San Juan, Puerto Rico. It was over 100 degrees at the outdoor baseball stadium by the time of the fight at 2pm and Laguna forfeited his right to walk to the ring second as champion, so he could claim the corner that was in the shade. Jack Solomons, Buchanan's promoter, borrowed a parasol from a woman in the crowd to shade Buchanan in between rounds. "If I had to pick out one highlight it would be Laguna," said Buchanan. "British fighters didn't do those things at the time."

27th SEPTEMBER 1980

On one of the most shameful nights in British boxing history, 'Marvelous' Marvin Hagler was presented with the WBC world middleweight belt in a dressing room at Wembley Arena shortly after being escorted there by police due to crowd trouble. After stopping Alan Minter for the title, Hagler faced the most danger he had all night when some of the 12,000 crowd threw bottles into the ring and racially abused the American. In the weeks leading up to the fight, Minter was reported as saying: "I am not letting any black man take the title from me." Hagler made Minter pay. Minter waged a toe-to-toe war from the first bell, but was met with punishingly accurate blows as he tried to move in and it was not long before his face was covered in blood. After 45 seconds of the third round, with cuts around both eyes, the referee stopped it and missiles began landing in the ring.

28th SEPTEMBER 1976

Ken Norton was sure he had beaten Muhammad Ali again in their third meeting at the Yankee Stadium in New York. But it was Ali who got the narrow and disputed unanimous points verdict to retain his WBC-WBA world heavyweight titles. Ali dominated the last round behind his jab after Norton's corner told him to avoid any danger in the final round. Norton was left to regret his reticence when the scores of 8-7, 8-7 and 8-6 were announced. "I think even Ali knows I won it," said Norton. "I was robbed, what else can I say." Former US Marine Norton had broken Ali's jaw three years earlier in a points win, before losing on points six months later. Norton shared 39 rounds in total with Ali, with very little separating them. "I honestly thought he beat me in Yankee Stadium, but the judges gave it to me, and I'm grateful to them," Ali later said.

29th SEPTEMBER 1977

Earnie Shavers was a major player in the golden era of the heavyweight division and Muhammad Ali complimented him after their WBC-WBA world title fight by saying: "Earnie hit me so hard, he shook my kinfolk back in Africa." But Ali still did enough in a tenth defence to win a unanimous decision. It was Ali's ability to take a punch that earned him victory in a close fight with Shavers.

30th SEPTEMBER 1986

Lloyd Honeyghan, the Jamaica-born Londoner known as 'The Ragamuffin Man', stopped Donald Curry to become undisputed world welterweight champion in a massive shock in Atlantic City. Texan Curry, the world's best pound-for-pound fighter at the time, was stopped with a cut eye before the start of the seventh round after he failed to restrain the challenger's incessant attack. Honeyghan, flamboyant and never lacking in self-confidence, topped up his £110,000 purse with the £20,000 winnings from a 5-1 bet on himself. It was one of the biggest upsets by a British boxer overseas.

30th SEPTEMBER 2000

Felix Savon won a historic third Olympic heavyweight gold medal when he beat Russian Sultan Ibzagimov 21-13 on points in Sydney. The Cuban, who suffered a cut late in the bout, equalled the Olympic record of Hungarian Laszlo Papp and countryman Teofilo Stevenson with three boxing gold medals each.

BOXING
On This Day
History, Facts & Figures
from Every Day of the Year

October

1st OCTOBER 1975

Muhammad Ali described his experience in the 'Thriller in Manila' "as the closest thing to dying". Joe Frazier, the man who had broken Ali's unbeaten record four years earlier, was unyielding in his challenge for Ali's WBA and WBC world heavyweight titles in the final fight of their trilogy. Frazier dominated the middle rounds, before Ali's combinations slowed him down from the tenth. With both men nearing exhaustion, Ali let fly with a volley of punches in the 14th round. Frazier could hardly see out of swollen eyes and it was too much for Frazier's experienced trainer, Eddie Futch, who told his man: "Sit down, son. It's all over. No one will forget what you did here today." There was genuine animosity between the Americans with Ali calling Frazier an "Uncle Tom" and a "gorilla". They fought three times over 41 rounds. Before this fight, Frazier said: "It's real hatred. I don't want to knock him out, I want to take his heart out." Frazier never forgave Ali for his taunts.

2nd OCTOBER 1980

Larry Holmes wept in the ring and told Muhammad Ali "I love you, man" after forcing his one-time sparring partner's corner to retire him after ten rounds. It had been a one-sided contest during which Ali absorbed some punishing blows as he tried to become world heavyweight champion for a fourth time at Caesars Palace, Las Vegas. "When you fight a friend and a brother you can't get happiness. All I achieved was money," said WBC champion Holmes, who made $2.3 million to Ali's $8 million. Aged 38 and with his speech already slurred, public opinion overwhelmingly wanted Ali to retire. But he had one more fight before retiring when not long after it was revealed he was suffering from Parkinson's Disease.

3rd OCTOBER 1981

WBC lightweight champion Alexis Arguello ended the unbeaten 20-fight record of Ray Mancini when he stopped the 20-year-old American in the penultimate 14th round. Mancini began well but the more experienced Arguello took control in the later rounds and floored his challenger in the 13th and 14th rounds. Afterwards, Arguello tipped Mancini to one day be world champion – and seven months later he was after winning the WBA version of the title.

4th OCTOBER 1997

Lennox Lewis described Andrew Golota as a "misfit" and the Pole certainly looked in the wrong place during their world heavyweight title fight. Golota had got his shot at WBC champion Lewis on dubious grounds after twice being disqualified in fights against Riddick Bowe. It only lasted 95 seconds and the thrashing – featuring two knockdowns and just two punches landed by the challenger – was so bad that Golota collapsed 15 minutes after the drubbing and was revived by cardiopulmonary resuscitation. During a seizure in the dressing room, Golota had stopped breathing with no pulse for about half a minute.

5th OCTOBER 1988

Duke McKenzie's slick boxing finally broke the resistance of brave Filipino Rolando Bohol in the 11th round for the IBF flyweight belt. The south Londoner, who would go on to become Britain's first three-weight world champion since Bob Fitzsimmons, was well ahead on points and after flooring Bohol twice in the 11th the towel was thrown in late in the 11th at Wembley. McKenzie stylishly out-boxed Bohol from start to finish and afterwards was so overwhelmed with emotion that he could hardly speak during an interview with the BBC's Harry Carpenter. Within a year, McKenzie had lost the title to Northern Irishman Dave 'Boy' McAuley.

6th OCTOBER 2007

For a while, Manny Pacquiao's form over Mexican fighters earned him the nickname the Mexi-cutioner but he had to be content with a gritty points win in his rematch with Marco Antonio Barrera. The Filipino stopped Barrera in the 11th round of their first fight four years previously, but this time the Mexican stayed on his feet in the super-featherweight fight in Las Vegas. "It was different from our first fight," said Pacquiao. "I knew he'd have to box me, and that's what he did." Barrera was docked a point for hitting Pacquiao on a break in the 11th round and finished up losing a wide unanimous verdict. "I got too caught up in the action," said Barrera. "I probably shouldn't have stayed in those exchanges as long as I did." It was still an improved performance by Barrera, 33, from their first one-sided fight and afterwards he announced his retirement. "Honestly, this was my last fight," he said. As is often the case, Barrera returned for another five fights.

7th OCTOBER 1927

Tommy Loughran's reign as world light-heavyweight champion started when he unanimously outpointed veteran Mike McTigue in a fight that would be a turning point in contrasting ways for both fighters. McTigue, a farmer's son born in County Clare who moved to America aged 16, was nearly 35 by the time of this fight at Madison Square Garden that was officially his first defence of his second reign as champion. McTigue had been curiously awarded the title after Jack Delaney had relinquished it following his withdrawal from a scheduled defence against McTigue in August. McTigue's fortunes slumped after this loss, a third defeat in four fights with Loughran, and three years later had his licence withdrawn because of his losing form.

8th OCTOBER 2005

So good was their brutal first fight that José Luis Castillo and Diego Corrales were paid to do it again five months later. The rematch lived up to expectations, but Castillo's victory was tarnished. Mexican Castillo was castigated for weighing in 3½lbs over the lightweight limit and he put the extra bulk to good use. After three toe-to-toe rounds that were in keeping with the fierce intensity of their first fight, Corrales was floored by a stunning left early in the fourth. Corrales wobbled to his feet at the count of nine, but could not continue. As Castillo missed the weight, his WBC and WBO lightweight belts were not on the line.

9th OCTOBER 1993

Three years after Brighton eccentric Chris Eubank had won the world middleweight title fight against fellow Briton Nigel Benn, the bitter rivals met again in front of 42,000 at Old Trafford and 16.5 million TV viewers in a WBC-WBO world super-middleweight title fight. After 15 rounds of a pulsating see-saw scrap, it seemed that Benn had edged it. The judges thought otherwise, awarding a draw.

9th OCTOBER 1985

Londoner Mark Kaylor and Coventry's Errol Christie got their British middleweight title fight started early with a vicious brawl at the press conference to announce their forthcoming clash. Christie claimed Kaylor racially insulted him. There were calls for the fight to be scrapped because it was too racially charged but it went ahead and Kaylor recovered from a knockdown to win with no crowd trouble at Wembley Arena.

10th OCTOBER 1962

Fighting Harada pulled off a big shock when he won the WBA flyweight title with an 11th round knockout of Pone Kingpetch in Tokyo. Kingpetch had become Thailand's first world champion two years earlier while Harada was only 19 and had been a professional just two years. But in a rematch in Thailand three months later, the Japanese boxer lost the belt in a first defence on points. Harada would reign longer as world bantamweight champion later in the 1960s and Kingpetch would go on to become a three-time world flyweight champion.

11th OCTOBER 1988

Not many took notice when a 23-year-old, who had recently been released from prison after serving nearly five years for robbery, lost on his professional debut. After losing a four-round decision to Clinton Mitchell, Bernard Hopkins did not box for another 16 months but he was to go on to become the most successful middleweight in history, making a record-breaking 20 world title defences before stepping up a division and becoming the oldest world champion in history.

11th OCTOBER 1997

The longest reign of a British world champion began when Joe Calzaghe outpointed Chris Eubank in Sheffield for the WBO super-middleweight title. The belt would stay in the Welshman's possession for nearly 11 years and for 21 defences. Four years after his professional debut, Calzaghe faced fellow Briton Eubank for the vacant title and made an excellent start when he floored the former champion in the first round. But Eubank got up to go the distance with 25-year-old Calzaghe after taking the fight at just two weeks' notice.

12th OCTOBER 1978

Rahway State Prison in New Jersey was the bizarre venue when inmate James Scott beat Eddie Gregory (who later became known as Eddie Mustafa Muhammad and won the world title). In front of 500 fellow inmates at a maximum-security prison, Scott unanimously out-pointed Gregory, the No 1 contender for the world title. But Scott, who was incarcerated for armed robbery, never got his shot at the title and a year later was dropped from the rankings while Gregory went on to win the WBA world light-heavyweight title in 1980. Scott, aged 57, was released from prison in 2005 after serving 28 years.

13th OCTOBER 1937

Benny Lynch summoned up one glorious night before his career was prematurely cut short when he stopped Peter Kane in the 13th round in front of 40,000 at Shawfield Stadium in Glasgow. Lynch, 24, was at the peak of his powers for one final night as the world's best flyweight and he dropped his game 19-year-old challenger in the first round. Kane, a blacksmith from the Lancashire town of Golborne, battled back before Lynch's relentless punching overwhelmed him in the 13th round and he finished the fight draped over the bottom rope. Lynch was still champion but he would soon lose his battle with the bottle. The following year, Kane won the vacant world flyweight title and Lynch was finished. Nine years after his win over Kane, Lynch was dead due to his bad lifestyle.

14th OCTOBER 1936

In Freddie Mills's first year as a professional, he enjoyed a quick one round knockout of Jack Scott at Westover Ice Rink in Bournemouth. But when Mills went to the promoter asking for his purse, he was told he had not earned it yet. Mills, a future world light-heavyweight champion, had to face Scott again three hours later at the end of the show. This time Mills got the job done even quicker in the first round.

15th OCTOBER 1910

World middleweight champion Stanley Ketchel was shot dead by the lover of the woman who was cooking him breakfast. After a win over heavyweight Jim Smith, Ketchel went to a ranch in Missouri that belonged to Colonel R P Dickerson. The cook, Goldie Smith, was preparing 24-year-old Ketchel breakfast when a ranch hand named Walter Dipley shot him dead. Dipley and Smith, who may have been married, were found guilty of murder and robbery the following year. When he was informed of Ketchel's death, the boxer's manager

Willus Britt said: "Start counting to ten over the boy, he'll get up." Stanislaus Kiecal was born to a Russian father of Polish stock and a 14-year-old Polish-American mother. He grew up in Grand Rapids and became a hobo, running away from home aged 14. Drifting from job to job, Ketchel was a boozer, gambler and womaniser who once accidentally shot his trainer. Despite his profligate lifestyle, he won the world middleweight title aged 21.

16th OCTOBER 1987

As undisputed champion aged 21, Mike Tyson seemed invincible and debates were raging as to whether he was the best heavyweight in history after he stopped Tyrell Biggs in the seventh round in Atlantic City. Biggs's flicking jab from long range defused Tyson's usual explosive start but the champion caught up with him in the seventh. Biggs was up at nine from the first knockdown but moments later ended up crashing into the ring post with his legs in the air from a series of hooks. Victory – the first defence as undisputed champion of all three governing bodies – was satisfying for Tyson who was insulted by Biggs after he qualified for the 1984 Olympics and Tyson didn't. "He talked so much, he didn't show any class or respect," said Tyson about Biggs' pre-fight comment. "I wanted to make him pay with his health for what he said. I wanted to do it slowly. I wanted him to remember this for a long time."

17th OCTOBER 1969

Emile Griffith showed there was still life in him at 31 when he recovered from a third round knockdown to take world welterweight champion José Nápoles the distance in Los Angeles. Nápoles's faster hands ensured the decision was never in doubt but Griffith rallied in the later rounds.

17th OCTOBER 1973

Revenge was sweet and swift for Ben Villaflor as he knocked out Kuniaki Shibata in the first round to regain the WBA super-featherweight title. Hawaii-based Filipino Villaflor lost a points decision to Japan's Shibata earlier in the year but one punch was all it took to finish off his rival with a crunching left hook to the chin after one minute and 56 seconds in the rematch in front of his home fans in Honolulu.

18th OCTOBER 1991

Tommy Morrison, the latest Great White Hope, saw victory in his WBO world heavyweight title fight with Ray Mercer slip from his grasp as his fellow American forced a savage fifth round stoppage. Unbeaten Morrison – known for starring in *Rocky V* – had stopped 24 of his 28 victims but Mercer, a former Army drill sergeant, shrugged off a sluggish start to scramble Morrison's senses early in the fifth. Morrison retired in 1996 after being diagnosed with HIV and died in 2013, aged 44.

19th OCTOBER 1985

A pulsating battle came down to which exhausted fighter could peel themselves off the canvas in the 12th round when Lee Roy Murphy and Chisanda Mutti met in Monte Carlo. Zambian Mutti had boxed himself into the lead against American Murphy, the IBF world cruiserweight champion who was floored from a flurry of blows in the ninth. Yet Mutti's domination rapidly evaporated and by the tenth he looked a spent force. Mutti survived a knockdown in the 11th but when both went down from rights halfway through the 12th, it was Murphy who was able to get to his feet with the help of the ropes. When Mutti was counted out, Murphy was leaning against a corner post dazed and too tired to celebrate.

20th OCTOBER 1954

Johnny Saxton's 15-round unanimous points decision win over Kid Gavilan for the world welterweight title in Philadelphia left a stench. Twenty of the 22 ringside reporters gave it to Cuban Gavilan and the suspicion was it had been fixed, with New York bookmakers refusing bets on Saxton before the fight. Mobster Frank 'Blinky' Palermo, who was jailed in 1961 for corruption in boxing, managed Saxton while Gavilan was also controlled by the Mob and also profited from a controversial decision over Billy Graham.

21st OCTOBER 1953

Randy Turpin could not reproduce the quality he showed in both fights against Sugar Ray Robinson when he was dropped twice on his way to a points defeat to Bobo Olson. Robinson had vacated the world middleweight title, leaving Olson and Turpin to dispute the belt at Madison Square Garden, and it was the Hawaiian who looked sharper. Turpin had been distracted in the weeks before the fight over a tempestuous affair with Adele Daniels. Randy and brother Dick fell out over the scandal, leading to Dick walking away from Randy's corner during the Olson fight. A day after the fight Randy was arrested on charges of raping and assaulting Daniels before eventually settling out of court. Turpin, a national hero two years previously, was slammed by the British press for his display against Olson; the *Daily Express* headline was 'HE'S LET US DOWN' and the scandal with Adele Daniels was reported in every lurid detail.

22nd OCTOBER 1968

Britain's Chris Finnegan, an out-of-work builder's labourer, beat future world champion Mate Parlov, of Yugoslavia, on points in the Olympic middleweight quarter-final in Mexico City. It would be one of Finnegan's best wins in the ring. Finnegan went on to win Olympic gold and said: "I feel I've done something different. For once I'm not just a silly old bricklayer." Finnegan turned professional, won the British and European light-heavyweight titles, was knocked out by world champion Bob Foster in the 14th round in 1972 and retired in 1975 due to a detached retina after an epic encounter with Johnny Frankham.

23rd OCTOBER 1962

Nigerian Dick Tiger claimed his first world title when he survived a last round onslaught from Gene Fullmer at Candlestick Park in San Francisco. Fullmer had beaten the likes of Sugar Ray Robinson, Florentino Fernandez and Benny 'Kid' Paret leading up to his fight with Tiger for the vacant WBA middleweight title. Tiger moved to Britain and started his career while working in a paint factory. He lost the first four fights of his career but had been based in New York four years by the time he faced Fuller. The pair got to know each other pretty well since they fought three times in ten months, with a draw followed by a seventh round win for Tiger that ended Fullmer's career in August 1963.

24th OCTOBER 2013

To the relief of aspiring heavyweights – and many boxing fans bored with the heavyweight division – Vitali Klitschko, the reigning WBC world heavyweight champion, declared his intention to run for Ukrainian president in the March 2015 elections and so end his dominant reign. The 42–year-old had swatted all comers in an era light on talent in the heavyweight division. Vitali, like his brother Wladimir, will not be remembered as being one of the most entertaining world heavyweight champions but they were never lacking in class or dignity. In two reigns as world champion, Vitali made two defences of the WBO belt and 11 as WBC champion after taking four years out with a knee injury (2004-08).

25th OCTOBER 1968

Former world middleweight and light-heavyweight champion Dick Tiger and Frankie DePaula were involved in a classic ten-round title eliminator that saw both touch down twice. Tiger was twice decked in the second round, but his senses returned and he then dumped DePaula on the canvas twice in the third round at Madison Square Garden. Despite losing the decision, it was DePaula who got a shot at world light-heavyweight champion Bob Foster three months later. DePaula was stopped in a round amid theories the fight was fixed. Within a year of losing to Tiger, DePaula was in court on charges of stealing copper and hijacking and within two years he had been shot dead.

26th OCTOBER 1951

Rising star Rocky Marciano was left in tears and apologising by the end of his eighth round win over former world heavyweight champion Joe Louis at Madison Square Garden. Louis had been Marciano's hero and the Italian-American had reluctantly fought the balding 37-year-old who was pressured into a comeback by an unpaid tax bill of more than $300,000. "He doesn't fight according to the book, but he hit me with a library," said Louis of Marciano. In the changing room, Sugar Ray Robinson was crying at seeing Louis – his one-time idol – so convincingly beaten, as were members of the press. The following year, Marciano was world champion.

27th OCTOBER 1949

France was left in mourning at the news that Marcel Cerdan, lover of Édith Piaf and former world middleweight champion, had been killed in a plane crash. He was 33. Algerian-born Cerdan, married with three children, fell for French singer Piaf in the summer of 1948 shortly before he won the world title from Tony Zale. Cerdan lost the title to Jake LaMotta the following year and before he began training for a rematch with LaMotta he agreed to Piaf's request to visit her in New York, where she was on tour. But Cerdan's plane crashed over the Azores, Portugal, killing all on board. Piaf – famous for her song 'Non, je ne regrette rien' – blamed herself for asking Cerdan to visit her despite the boxer's fear of flying and she fell into a deep, drug and alcohol-fuelled depression.

28th OCTOBER 1978

English referee Harry Gibbs stopped the WBA super-bantamweight title fight in Puerto Rican Wilfredo Gomez's favour in the fifth round after Mexican Carlos Zarate's corner threw in the towel. The pair had the highest knockout ratio between them in the history of world title fights, with Gomez stopping all 21 victims in 22 fights (he drew on his professional debut) and Zarate halting 54 of his 55 opponents. Zarate entered the fight weight drained after needing four attempts to make the weight.

29th OCTOBER 1948

It was remarkable that Willie Pep was in the ring at all to defend his world featherweight title as he suffered a broken leg, cracked vertebrae and a chest injury in a plane crash on 5 January, 1947. But he returned to the ring just five months later to resume his reign. Pep was so elusive it was claimed you could throw a handful of rice at him and you would still miss, but Sandy Saddler had no problem hitting him at Madison Square Garden. Pep had been the featherweight champion for nearly six years when he faced Saddler for the first time. Pep was three inches smaller than Saddler, who comfortably picked him off and floored him twice in the third round, then knocked him out in the fourth with a left hook to the jaw. It was the second defeat in 140 bouts for Pep, who would avenge the loss four months later but suffered two more stoppage losses to Saddler. After

MUHAMMAD ALI USING HIS ROPE-A-DOPE TACTICS AGAINST GEORGE FOREMAN IN 1974

winning the title, Saddler dominated the division until he was forced to retire while still champion in 1957 due to an eye injury sustained in a car crash.

29th OCTOBER 1960

Cassius Clay, later to become Muhammad Ali, made his professional debut with a unanimous six round points decision over Tunney Hunsaker in Louisville, Kentucky. Clay, the Olympic light-heavyweight gold medallist, earned $2,000. "He's awfully good for an 18-year-old and as fast as a middleweight," said Hunsaker, a 30-year-old police chief who got $300.

30th OCTOBER 1974

'The Rumble in the Jungle' is perhaps the most famous fight in history and helped make Muhammad Ali a legend. Ali employed his own cunning rope-a-dope tactics to tame big-hitting champion George Foreman and regain the world heavyweight title at the age of 32 via an eighth round stoppage in Kinshasa, Zaire. Foreman was making a third title defence after blasting away the likes of Joe Frazier and Ken Norton – both victorious over Ali – in two rounds each, stopping 37 of his 40 victims. Ali was four years into a comeback after three and a half years out due to his exile for refusing the draft for the Vietnam War. He was slower than before but could still rely on his intelligence, courage and strength of mind to dismantle another ring monster. Ali looked on the point of collapse after absorbing so much punishment through his rope-a-dope tactics of resting with his back against the ropes and deliberately allowing Foreman to punch him, leaning out of range and blocking some shots with his arms and gloves. By the sixth and seventh rounds, Foreman was drained of energy and had punched himself out. "He would just lay back on the ropes and let me pummel him and then he'd whisper in my ear 'Is that all you got George?' Trouble was, it was," said Foreman. Late in the eighth round, with Foreman on rubbery legs, Ali suddenly slid off the ropes to floor his fellow American with a snaking left hook followed by a straight right. Foreman was sent spinning to the canvas and was counted out. "I said I was the Greatest and I proved it, so never make me underdog again, until I'm 50 and then you might get me," said Ali after the fight.

31st OCTOBER 1998

Naseem Hamed was booed for his showboating during a points win over fellow Briton Wayne McCullough in Atlantic City that did nothing to enhance his popularity in America. WBO featherweight champion Hamed had promised to stop former world champion McCullough in three rounds, but the Belfast boxer's granite chin ensured the Sheffield fighter was taken the distance. Hamed faced criticism for the display and McCullough said: "He didn't hurt me, and I'm only a bantamweight. He ran from me."

BOXING
On This Day
History, Facts & Figures
from Every Day of the Year

November

1st NOVEMBER 1980

Jim Watt made a fourth and final defence of his WBC world lightweight title when he stopped Oklahoma's Sean O'Grady on cuts in the 12th round at the Kelvin Hall in Watt's native Glasgow. Watt, 32, employed a clever strategy against the dangerman who had accounted for 65 of his 75 opponents within the distance; the Scot kept out of range until the later rounds when a cut forced the stoppage. But it was Watt's head, rather than his fists, that caused the decisive cut. O'Grady, 21, suffered a gash on his forehead caused by a butt in the tenth round (unseen by the referee) which prompted the stoppage two rounds later.

2nd NOVEMBER 1984

Carlos Santos came perilously close to losing his IBF light-middleweight title fight with fellow Puerto Rican Mark Medal in the 14th round when he found himself on the floor. Santos, cut over the right eye, was in retreat when Medal finally caught up with him to land a big left hook. But Santos got up and survived the rest of the round and the 15th to earn a decision (153½-152½) over Medal, who himself visited the canvas in the first round. Santos's work in the first ten rounds was enough to get him the verdict.

3rd NOVEMBER 2007

Welshman Joe Calzaghe was crowned the division's No 1 after adding Dane Mikkel Kessler's WBA and WBC belts to his WBO strap via a unanimous points decision. After a pulsating tenth round, Calzaghe finished stronger to win by scores of 117-111, 116-112 and 116-112 in front of 50,000 fans in Cardiff. Kessler later revealed he fought with an injury and it was Calzaghe's 21st and last WBO defence before stepping up to light-heavyweight for his last two fights.

3rd NOVEMBER 2001

Zab Judah went berserk after referee Jay Nady waved off his world light-welterweight fight with Australia-based Russian Kostya Tszyu. New Yorker Judah was caught heavily in round two before being put on his back by a right hand with a second to go of the round. He quickly got to his feet only to drunkenly lurch about the ring until falling over, prompting Nady to call it off. Judah put a glove in Nady's face and then threw a stool across the ring.

4th NOVEMBER 2006

Despite injuring his right hand halfway through the fight, Floyd Mayweather Jr won nearly every round to earn a unanimous points decision to take the title from WBC welterweight champion Carlos Baldomir. The American was limited to using just his left hand for the last three rounds.

5th NOVEMBER 1994

George Foreman knelt down in a corner of the ring and began praying immediately after Michael Moorer was counted out. Foreman's prayers had been answered with a tenth round knockout and he was IBF-WBA world heavyweight champion again at the age of 45. Trainer Angelo Dundee, the cornerman of Foreman's opponent Muhammad Ali in 'The Rumble in the Jungle', told Foreman to "knock this guy down, you're behind baby" as the fleshy veteran shuffled out for the tenth round. He looked laboured but Moorer's lazy defence permitted a right hand to land flush on the chin and the 26-year-old was deposited dazed on the canvas. Foreman became the oldest boxer to hold the world heavyweight title 20 years and one week since he had lost to Ali. Foreman was wearing the same red shorts he wore against Ali. "Too old, too fat, but world champion," the punching preacher said.

6th NOVEMBER 1993

When Fan Man interrupted a world heavyweight title fight by dropping into the ring on a motorised hang glider, it became one of the most ludicrous moments in boxing history. However, Riddick Bowe did not find it funny and the stunt could well have cost him the fight. James Miller, AKA Fan Man, had circled the outdoor arena at Caesars Palace in Las Vegas before descending into the ring during the seventh round of Bowe's rematch with Evander Holyfield. Bowe and Holyfield stopped trading blows and stood in astonishment. Bowe's entourage then attacked Miller. "It was a heavyweight fight and I was the only guy who got knocked out," Miller said. "It was a conspiracy," Bowe said. "They knew eventually Evander Holyfield would fade. They had this cat up in the air waiting for him." It caused a 22-minute delay and Holyfield went on to win by a majority decision. Miller hanged himself by the cords of his parachute in Alaska aged 39 in 2003.

7th NOVEMBER 2009

It looked like a scene from *Gulliver's Travels* but luckily for David Haye the 7ft, 22-stone giant in front of him was one of the worst world heavyweight champions in history. Russian Nikolai Valuev still started favourite in Nuremberg due to his size and weight advantages, but Haye's tactics of hit and run exposed lumbering Valuev's lack of boxing finesse. Valuev – the biggest heavyweight champion in history who had a massive seven-stone weight advantage and was nearly a foot taller than Haye – was left flailing and in the last round was even wobbled by a combination. Valuev never boxed again after Londoner Haye relieved him of his WBA title to become a two-weight world champion.

8th NOVEMBER 2008

Joe Calzaghe had to climb off the canvas for the second successive fight in America to ensure his unbeaten record remained intact. A faded Roy Jones Jr gave the Welshman a shock in the first round of their light-heavyweight bout, but Calzaghe got up to win convincingly on points – 118-109 on all three scorecards – at Madison Square Garden. A few months later, Calzaghe retired after a 46-fight unbeaten career.

8th NOVEMBER 2014

Bernard Hopkins, two months short of his 50th birthday and the oldest ever world champion, took a hammering off Sergey Kovalev in a world light-heavyweight title unification clash. Hopkins was floored in the first and took some worrying blows in the last minute of a bout his unbeaten Russian opponent won by scores of 120-107 and 120-106. Afterwards, WBA-IBF-WBO champion Kovalev urged Hopkins to retire. "Asking me to fight again right now is like asking a woman who was just in nine hours of labour to have another baby," said Hopkins.

9th NOVEMBER 1996

Nigel Benn had been one of the most exciting and popular British boxers in the modern era but after his last appearance in the ring he was booed. The Londoner, a world champion at middleweight and super-middleweight, retired on his stool with an ankle injury at the end of the sixth round against Irishman Steve Collins in Manchester. When Benn – known as the Dark Destroyer – addressed the crowd on the microphone after the fight, he was jeered by the 20,000 fans who chanted, "What a load of rubbish".

10th NOVEMBER 1983

Marvin Hagler finished the fight with blood pouring down his face and an eye swollen shut, but his work in the last two rounds was enough to outpoint Roberto Duran with all three world middleweight titles on the line. The American was heading for a points defeat on the judges' scorecards after 13 rounds but staged a late rally to see off Panamanian Duran by scores of 144-142, 146-145, and 144-143. "He came to tear my head off, but when he saw that I could hit him hard, with strength, he got scared and became a coward," said an unbowed Duran. "That's why he didn't take too many chances and mix it up with me."

11th NOVEMBER 2006

Laila Ali made her dad Muhammad a proud man as she stopped Shelley Burton in the fourth round to defend her WBC women's super-middleweight title at Madison Square Garden in New York. Muhammad Ali, suffering from Parkinson's Disease, entered the arena driving a golf buggy to cheers of the crowd. It was the last time he saw his daughter fight as she retired after her next bout.

12th NOVEMBER 1982

After a ferocious duel displaying breathtaking courage, Alexis Arguello failed in his attempt to become boxing's first four-weight world champion when the accumulation of punishment from Aaron Pryor took its toll in the 14th round. Pryor had notorious trainer Panama Lewis in his corner and in between rounds 13 and 14 Lewis was caught on the broadcaster's microphones saying to his cutman: "Give me the other bottle, the one I mixed." Pryor was sharp in the 14th round and the fight was stopped after he landed a series of unanswered punches. A post-fight urine test was not carried out and Pryor, angered at the cries of foul play, took the rematch – and beat Arguello in ten rounds.

13th NOVEMBER 1982

South Korean Deuk-Koo Kim died four days after being knocked out in the 14th round against Ray 'Boom Boom' Mancini for the WBA lightweight title. Kim's mother committed suicide three months later, as did the fight's referee Richard Green the following year. The WBC world governing body decided to reduce fights from 15 rounds to 12 after this death and five years later the WBA and IBF followed suit.

13th NOVEMBER 1999

Lennox Lewis became Britain's first undisputed world heavyweight champion since Bob Fitzsimmons's reign ended 97 years earlier with a unanimous points decision over American Evander Holyfield. The WBC, WBA and IBF belts were on the line at the Thomas & Mack Center in Las Vegas, with gross receipts of $16.9million.

14th NOVEMBER 1947

Jake LaMotta took a dive against Billy Fox, going down in the fourth round, because he believed he would get a world middleweight title shot for doing so. LaMotta had grown impatient at being kept out of title contention because until this fight he had refused to work with the Mob, who largely controlled American boxing at the time. Betting odds switched from the big favourite LaMotta to Fox on the day of the fight and hours before the first bell worried bookies stopped taking bets. Fox challenged Gus Lesnevich for the world light-heavyweight title in his next fight while LaMotta was briefly suspended after two investigations into the fix. LaMotta claimed he had injured his back in training and it was another two years before he got his shot at the NBA version of the world title.

15th NOVEMBER 1984

Never before have so many careers of future boxing stars been launched on one night under the same roof. The US boxing team had plundered a record nine gold medals, one silver and one bronze from the Los Angeles Olympic Games earlier in the year. Promoter Dan Duva's event – titled 'A Night of Gold' – included four of those gold medallists making their professional debuts: teenager Meldrick Taylor, Pernell Whitaker, Mark Breland and Tyrell Biggs. Silver

LENNOX LEWIS LANDS A JAB ON HIS WAY TO VICTORY OVER EVANDER HOLYFIELD IN 1999

medallist Virgil Hill and bronze medallist Evander Holyfield also made their punch-for-pay starts on the same bill at Madison Square Garden. All six made successful starts to their paid careers that would see all of them go on to win world titles.

16th NOVEMBER 1927

Tiger Flowers died aged 32 four days after the last of his 159 bouts due to complications that arose during surgery to remove scar tissue from his right eye. Flowers won the non-title bout against Leo Gates by a fourth round stoppage – his 19th bout in 1927 – but was admitted to hospital after. An anaesthetic overdose is one possible reason for his death. Religious Flowers had lost the world middleweight title to Mickey Walker 11 months previously after twice beating Harry Greb for the belt. Greb had also died in surgery to correct an injury the year before Flowers's death.

17th NOVEMBER 1972

Roberto Duran, one of the most crowd-pleasing boxers in modern boxing history, suffered his first career defeat to Esteban DeJesus in the first of their three fights. Puerto Rican DeJesus floored Panamanian Duran in the opening moments before earning a ten round unanimous points decision. Duran had won the WBA lightweight title from Ken Buchanan five months earlier, but the belt was not on the line. Duran would go on to beat DeJesus in two world lightweight title fights.

18th NOVEMBER 1990

There have been few rivalries more intense than that between Britons Nigel Benn and Chris Eubank. Unconventional Eubank, originally from south London with an odd dress sense who was making the second defence of his WBO middleweight title, said before their first of two meetings: "I find the man intolerable, he has no class as far as I see it." Benn, a former soldier from east London, replied: "I detest him, I really do. It's no joke. I can't stand him." They could not even look at each other in TV interviews or at press conferences, so sat with their backs facing each other. Benn sabotaged Eubank's ring walk music, cutting off Tina Turner's 'Simply the Best' at the NEC in Birmingham. But Eubank had the last laugh. Eubank was given a count in the eighth but appeared to slip on water in a corner and it was Benn who was in real trouble a round later. After withstanding Benn's body shots, Eubank sent Benn staggering to the ropes from a straight right and referee Richard Steele stopped the fight. As Benn was returning to his senses, Eubank was proposing to his girlfriend Karron during a television interview.

19th NOVEMBER 1943

Beau Jack had an entertaining, fast-fighting style that earned him top billing at Madison Square Garden 21 times, one of which was the rematch with Bob Montgomery. Jack, from Georgia, earned a unanimous decision to regain the world lightweight title he had lost to Montgomery on points ten months earlier. Jack was an exceptionally fit fighter who learned to use his fists in the cruel Battle Royals, when half a dozen blindfolded black children punched each other until one was left standing for small change from a white audience.

20th NOVEMBER 1931

Italian-American Tony Canzoneri and Cuban Kid Chocolate maintained a furious pace for 15 rounds until Canzoneri was given the split points decision in the world lightweight title fight. It ended a dream year for former featherweight champion Canzoneri, who also defended his world light-welterweight belt with this entertaining win over his Cuban opponent. The rematch two years later was just as entertaining but was over in two rounds with Canzoneri delivering a knockout.

21st NOVEMBER 1987

"That Mexican is a cheat and a coward and you only have to look in his eyes to know he is a very frightened man," said Edwin Rosario of Julio Cesar Chavez. The challenger was equally complimentary about his opponent: "There is a resentment between the Mexicans and the Puerto Ricans, the reason being the Puerto Ricans talk too much and they almost always come out looking bad." Chavez ensured WBA lightweight champion Rosario ended up looking bad with an indefatigable attack that left Rosario leaking blood all over the canvas. In round 11, Rosario was trapped in a corner while Chavez whacked him to the body and gradually the fight drained out of the champion.

With his left eye closed and unable to see Chavez's unforgiving right hands, his corner threw in the towel towards the end of the 11th. Chavez, Mexico's biggest boxing hero and then aged 25, was a two-weight world champion after this one-sided masterclass.

22nd NOVEMBER 1986

Mike Tyson seemed one of boxing's most frightening forces after he reduced Trevor Berbick to a staggering drunk, out of his senses, in round two. 'Iron' Mike, a former street thug from New York, knocked down Berbick twice in round two and the Jamaican's spaghetti legs twice betrayed him as he tried to stay upright from the second knockdown. Aged 20 years and five months, Tyson became the youngest ever world heavyweight champion after lifting the WBC belt in Las Vegas. Moments before the fight, Muhammad Ali was called into the ring and wandered over to the unbeaten challenger. "Avenge me," said Ali, who lost to Berbick in 1981 in his last ever fight. "Every punch I threw with bad intentions," said Tyson. "I aimed for his ear. I wanted to bust his eardrum."

23rd NOVEMBER 1974

Ruben Olivares ran out of steam in a first defence of his WBA featherweight title to allow Alexis Arguello to separate him from his senses in the 13th round. Mexican Olivares thought he could stop Nicaraguan Arguello in the 12th but only succeeded in punching himself out. In the following round, Arguello turned the tables and dropped Olivares with a left hook. Olivares slowly got up only to be quickly finished by the Explosive Thin Man, who was making his US debut.

24th NOVEMBER 2012

Former world light-welterweight and welterweight champion Ricky Hatton insisted he had no regrets about his comeback, despite ending it flat on his back. After problems with alcohol, drugs and depression Hatton had been left contemplating suicide before cleaning up his act and embarking on a ring return. After three years out of action, Hatton's timing was off and Ukrainian Vyacheslav Senchenko attacked the body until Hatton was counted out in front of his saddened home fans in Manchester in round nine.

24th NOVEMBER 1990

Herol 'Bomber' Graham, one of the best British boxers never to win a world title, was knocked out cold in the fourth round by Julian Jackson in a Spanish bullring. The normally elusive Sheffield boxer was in utter control of the vacant WBC middleweight title bout and Jackson was given only another round because his eyes were swelling shut. But the American launched a vicious right hook against the ropes to knock out Graham.

25th NOVEMBER 1903

In a feat to lift the spirits of any forty-something, Bob Fitzsimmons became boxing's first three-weight world champion when he out-pointed George Gardener over 20 rounds for the world light-heavyweight crown aged 40. Fitzsimmons, who left Cornwall in childhood to live in New Zealand, had already won world titles at middleweight and heavyweight before he reinvented himself in the new light-heavyweight division. Known as Ruby Robert, and less kindly The Freckled Freak, Fitzsimmons forced four knockdowns against Irish-born Gardener, who was 14 years his junior, in San Francisco.

25th NOVEMBER 1980

Sugar Ray Leonard got revenge over Roberto Duran by getting his fearsome rival to do the unthinkable: quit. Duran was a maniacal puncher with an insatiable appetite for violence who had turned their first fight earlier that year into a brawl, which he won on points. This time in New Orleans, Leonard relied on his silky skills and regained his welterweight crown in style as he left the Panamanian so out-boxed he told his corner: "No more". When Duran got back to his stool at the end of the eighth round frustrated at not being able to get to Leonard, he said: "No mas, no mas". "To make Roberto Duran quit seemed impossible," Leonard said. "It was better than knocking him out. I outclassed, humiliated and frustrated him. He couldn't take it mentally. I didn't hurt him or make him bleed. I just made him look a fool before millions."

26th NOVEMBER 1936

Billy Papke, who beat fellow American Stanley Ketchel for the world middleweight title in 1908 and lost a rematch two months later, shot and killed his estranged wife Edna moments before turning the gun on himself, aged 50.

27th NOVEMBER 2010

Outside in Helsinki the temperature was -20 degrees, but in the ring Carl Froch showed some of the hottest form of his life when he gave Arthur Abraham a boxing lesson. The Nottingham boxer won back the WBC super-middleweight title with a slick display of box-and-move that snuffed out the danger of hard-hitting Armenian Abraham. Froch cruised to a unanimous decision of 119-109, 120-108 and 120-108. But only a small live TV audience in the UK on a little-known cable channel saw it.

28th NOVEMBER 1980

Matthew Saad Muhammad knocked out Lotte Mwale with a stunning left uppercut that landed flush on the jaw and left his challenger flat out. The American was at the peak of his powers for this WBC world light-heavyweight title defence, which ended suddenly late in the fourth round. Saad Muhammad rated it the best punch he ever threw, and it was hard to disagree. Saad Muhammad felt his body punches set up the decisive attack, which was a right lead followed by a swinging, left uppercut. "I knocked out Mwale with body punches," said Muhammad. "The punch that finished him was a left uppercut, but the body punches slowed him down."

29th NOVEMBER 1999

The agony of losing his second and last world title shot only deepened for Billy Schwer when the following month it was revealed American Stevie Johnston had tested positive for the stimulant ephedrine for their WBC lightweight title fight at Wembley Arena. The Luton boxer had no complaints on the night after all three judges returned eight-point margins in favour of slick Johnston. But Schwer understandably felt aggrieved when WBC president Jose Sulaiman ruled no disciplinary action would be taken with Johnston as the drug-testing procedure had flouted the sanctioning body's rules. "That fight should have been declared a no-contest because Johnston cheated, it's as simple as that," said Schwer. Johnson said he took the substance inadvertently in a cold remedy and Schwer never fought for one of the four major world titles again, although did briefly hold the IBO light-welterweight belt.

30th NOVEMBER 1955

Carmen Basilio floored Tony DeMarco twice in the 12th and decisive round of their rematch in a first defence of the world welterweight title. It was the same outcome as their first fight earlier in the year, but their second bout was even more entertaining. Basilio, known as the Upstate Onion Picker because he used to work on his father's onion farm in Canastota, survived a torrid time in the seventh round, almost going down from a left hook, and was trailing on the judges' scorecards when he twice floored DeMarco in the 12th. The fight was stopped after the second knockdown.

Boxing On This Day

BOXING
On This Day

History, Facts & Figures
from Every Day of the Year

December

1st DECEMBER 2001

Anthony Mundine, the Australian former rugby league player who had been a professional boxer just 17 months, was heading for an unlikely points win against local icon Sven Ottke in Germany when in the tenth round he was knocked out by a right hand to the temple. Mundine did not sit up for five minutes after being caught by IBF super-middleweight king Ottke, who finished his career undefeated in 22 world title fights.

2nd DECEMBER 1896

There is no boxing referee more infamous than Wild West gunslinger Wyatt Earp, who disqualified Bob Fitzsimmons in the eighth round against Tom 'Sailor' Sharkey. Earp was the notorious former deputy marshal of Dodge City and Tombstone where he took part in the Gunfight at the OK Corral in 1881 that left three cowboys shot dead. In his life, Earp killed between eight to 30 outlaws. It therefore must have been disconcerting for British-born Fitzsimmons to be informed on the morning of the fight that Earp would be the third man in the ring. Earp even got into the ring with a six-shooter around his waist, until asked to remove it by a police captain after being booed by the 15,000 crowd in San Francisco. Fitzsimmons maintained control throughout and Sharkey hit the canvas following a left to the body in the eighth round, but Earp did not even issue a count. Instead, Earp ruled that Dundalk-born Sharkey had been the victim of a low blow and disqualified Fitzsimmons. Earp is believed to have been part of a betting ring that had invested heavily on Sharkey to win the eliminator to face James J Corbett for the world heavyweight title. After public outcry at the controversial decision, Fitzsimmons progressed to a world title shot a year later when the same punch earned him victory over Corbett. Earp never refereed again.

3rd DECEMBER 1982

Lupe Pintor came off the ropes to wobble Wilfredo Gomez with hooks and uppercuts in an enthralling third round, but the Mexican was ground down in the 14th round. Puerto Rican Gomez retained his WBC super-bantamweight title for the 17th time after a desperately close fight. Pintor tired and after getting up from a right hand in the 14th, was stopped on his feet by the referee.

4th DECEMBER 1998

Manny Pacquiao began his collection of world titles at flyweight when he stopped local hero Chatchai Sasakul in three rounds in Thailand. At this stage of his career, Pacquiao had only fought in his native Philippines, Japan and Thailand. Within a year of winning his first world title, Pac Man was dethroned after returning to Thailand to lose in three rounds to Medgoen Singsurat. But Pacquiao then teamed up with trainer Freddie Roach in Los Angeles and went on to win (WBC/WBA/IBF/WBO) world titles in seven weight divisions (not including the IBO light-welterweight title): flyweight, super-bantamweight, featherweight, super-featherweight, lightweight, welterweight and light-middleweight.

5th DECEMBER 1947

Joe Louis had to pull himself off the canvas twice before winning a narrow points decision over Jersey Joe Walcott to retain his world heavyweight title. Walcott floored Louis in the first and fourth rounds and the scare led to a rematch the following year when the champion again had to climb off the canvas twice before winning, this time by 11th round stoppage, in his 25th and final defence. This fight showed the vulnerabilities of the aging champion Louis, who was close to being stopped in the opening round by 10-1 underdog Walcott, who was also 33.

6th DECEMBER 1975

There can be few more intimidating places for a boxer to fight than in a bullring in Mexico City in front of 40,000 locals against a Mexican hero. That was the unenviable position East Ender John H Stracey found himself in when challenging Cuban-born José Nápoles for his WBC welterweight title. Stracey looked as though he was about to crumble like a tortilla chip when he was put on his backside by a left hook in the first round. But Stracey had previous knowledge of Nápoles and recovered to execute his game plan to perfection. Stracey had sparred with Nápoles three years previous when the Mexican idol had visited for a title defence. Stracey never forgot how the jab worked for him when he sparred with Nápoles and in the third round it was the Mexican resident who touched down. Stracey then inflicted a steady beating on the aging champion, who had been world-title holder on and off for the previous six years. Nápoles was stopped on a cut in the sixth round of his last fight and Stracey would go on to make a single defence.

7th DECEMBER 1906

Abe Attell, who ruled as world featherweight champion for nearly a decade in total, crushed Jimmy Walsh in nine rounds in his native California when the challenger's corner threw in the towel and referee Tommy Burns – the reigning world heavyweight champion – stopped the fight. Walsh's corner tried frantically to stop the slaughter in the previous round by throwing in the towel, but Walsh insisted he was OK before needing to be dragged back to his stool. The champion showed no mercy in the ninth and sunk Walsh with a right to the stomach and the towel was thrown in again.

8th DECEMBER 2007

With nearly a million people watching on pay-per-view TV, pound-for-pound king Floyd Mayweather Jr weathered an early storm from Manchester hero Ricky Hatton to execute a rare knockout. It was claimed 30,000 had followed Hatton to the Nevada desert to see him take on the world's best boxer for the WBC welterweight title. Some were at the weigh-in where Hatton screamed at them: "Let's f***ing have it!" But Mayweather was masterful, knocking out Hatton with a right hook in the tenth round at the MGM Grand in Las Vegas. "I slipped," joked Hatton, who admitted: "I needed to keep a cool head, but I was too gung-ho and you can't be against a boxer as good as him." In the next seven years, Mayweather would register just one more stoppage win and did not box again for 21 months after inflicting the first defeat in 44 fights for Hatton, who earned about $10million.

9th DECEMBER 1959

Sonny Liston showed why people were talking about him being the hardest hitting heavyweight since Joe Louis when he became the first person to stop German Willi Besmanoff, who was badly gashed around the right eye prompting the referee to halt the fight before the start of the seventh round. It was a significant victory in the menacing contender's rise to challenging for the world heavyweight title in 1962. Liston, from St Louis, was a brooding figure who learned to box during a two-year stint in prison for robbery. He returned to jail for six months in 1956 for assaulting a police officer and resisting arrest.

10th DECEMBER 2011

Amir Khan felt aggrieved after he was controversially outpointed by Lamont Peterson. The Bolton boxer complained about being deducted two points for pushing, a changed scorecard and the presence of a "mystery man in the hat" – later identified as Mustafa Ameen – following his split points defeat in Peterson's home city of Washington. To rub salt into the wound for Khan, Peterson subsequently tested positive for a banned substance that meant a rematch – set for May 2012 – was scrapped at late notice, costing Khan more money. Peterson failed a random urine test for taking testosterone, an anabolic steroid banned in boxing, before fighting Khan.

11th DECEMBER 1982

In a remarkable tale of bravery and triumphing over adversity, Bobby Chacon captured the WBC super-featherweight title from Rafael Limon nine months after contemplating suicide. Chacon had put a gun to his head following the suicide of his wife Valorie because he would not quit boxing. Chacon was left haunted by guilt and his life was at rock bottom when aged 31, with three children to support and seven years after he had lost his featherweight title, he met his Mexican rival for a fourth time. With his face bloodied and swollen, Chacon looked to be heading for defeat after being dropped in the third and tenth rounds. He was cut on the bridge of the nose and had to beg the ringside doctor to allow him to continue in the 12th round. Somehow, the American found the energy to go on the front foot for the remaining rounds and crucially decked Limon after two short rights to the jaw with 12 seconds left in the 15th and final round. It was enough to earn Chacon the close decision. "This is dedicated to my wife, if only she could be here with me," Chacon said after. "I told her this was all I wanted."

12th DECEMBER 1992

Dubbed 'The Brain versus the Beast' in a battle between the instinctive brawler and educated boxer, Nigel Benn stopped Nicky Piper in the 11th round to defend his WBC world super-middleweight title. Welshman Piper, who had a Mensa membership and an IQ of 153, was knocked down with a left hook and Benn then followed up to force the stoppage.

13th DECEMBER 1887

What was astonishing about Nonpareil Jack Dempsey's 45th round stoppage of John Reagan was not the length of the fight, but the fact that it took place in two locations. They got to the first venue on the shore of Long Island Sound by tug boat, but after 15 minutes they found themselves scrapping in the rising tide with snow falling. The boxers, officials and crowd then had to travel 25 miles before finding a suitable location to reassemble the ropes and continue the bout. Dempsey had his leg ripped open by Reagan's spiked shoes but wore his opponent down and Reagan's seconds retired their fighter at the end of the 44th round. Dempsey was known as Nonpareil because he was so dominant: he suffered just four defeats in his 67-bout career. Dempsey – real name John Kelly – was born in County Kildare and grew up in New York after his parents emigrated there in his childhood. His parents disliked boxing, so he assumed a different name. He died of tuberculosis five years later aged 32.

14th DECEMBER 2013

It was hard to have much sympathy with Adrien Broner as he fled the ring following a humbling points defeat to Argentine Marcos Maidana for the WBA welterweight title in Texas. The American had been his usual flash and arrogant self in the build-up to the fight, calling Maidana a "stepping stone", but was floored twice. Brash Broner found the end of his unbeaten record too much to take and ran out the arena to the sound of boos and drinks being thrown at him. It was Broner's second fight at welterweight after ruling as world lightweight champion.

15th DECEMBER 2001

Dariusz Michalczewski looked on course to smash the records of Joe Louis and Rocky Marciano after he stopped Richard Hall in the 11th round due to a large swelling by his challenger's eye to defend his WBO world light-heavyweight title. The Poland-born Germany-based boxer made three more successful defences to set a record number of world title defences at light-heavyweight (23) and was just two short of Joe Louis's record of most title defences across all divisions and one short of eclipsing Rocky Marciano's 49-0 unbeaten record when Julio Gonzalez caught up with him.

16th DECEMBER 2000

Joe Calzaghe stopped Richie Woodhall in the tenth round, but it was not the Welshman's classy defence of his WBO super-middleweight title that got the headlines but another fight on the same Sheffield bill. IBF featherweight champion Paul Ingle sustained life-threatening brain injuries after being stopped in the final round by Mbulelo Botile. Ingle was down in rounds 11 and 12 before he lost consciousness in an ambulance on the way to a local hospital. He needed brain surgery, which lasted two and a half hours and began only 45 minutes after he was knocked out, to remove a blood clot. Ingle never boxed again. He ballooned in weight and was left being reliant on a small disability pension and being cared for by his mother.

17th DECEMBER 1994

Bernard Hopkins failed for a second time at becoming world champion amid a hostile atmosphere in the centre of a bullring in front of 15,000 spectators in Ecuador. Segundo Mercado floored Hopkins in the fifth and seventh rounds, the first times the American had visited the canvas as a professional. He got up to draw on points with Mercado for the vacant IBF belt. The previous year, Hopkins had lost on points to Roy Jones Jr. But Hopkins, who turned professional aged 23 after serving almost five years in prison for robbery, began his historic reign as world middleweight champion in a rematch with Mercado in April 1995 by a seventh-round stoppage. Hopkins went on to make a record-breaking 20 world middleweight title defences.

18th DECEMBER 1993

Terry Norris lost his WBC light-middleweight title in an 11th defence when Jamaica-born Simon Brown knocked him out in the fourth round. In the biggest upset of the year, an out-of-sorts Norris was floored by a jab in the first round. Norris was wobbled in the third before going down in the fourth, but he got revenge and his title back in a rematch five months later by a landslide points decision.

19th DECEMBER 1997

The Sheffield featherweight Naseem Hamed made a thrilling American debut when he got off the canvas three times before stopping home hero Kevin Kelley in the fourth round in New York. The WBO featherweight champion was a curiosity to most fans in the US before this fight at Madison Square Garden and after was one of the biggest personalities in world boxing. Hamed hit the canvas in the first, second, and fourth rounds with Kelley dropped in the second and twice in the fourth round. Hamed, who would somersault over the top rope to enter the ring and could never be accused of lacking confidence, made six more world title defences before being embarrassingly dismantled by Mexican Marco Antonio Barrera in April 2001.

20th DECEMBER 1963

Rubin 'Hurricane' Carter's potential to go beyond just being a middleweight contender was highlighted by his first round demolition of reigning world welterweight champion Emile Griffith. Those 133 seconds of the non-title catchweight bout, which saw Griffith floored twice, would be the best achievement of Carter's unfulfilled career. A year later, Carter lost a unanimous decision to Joey Giardello for the world title, but there was never another chance at glory. Carter's boxing career was terminated by an event three years after inflicting Griffith's first stoppage loss. Carter was wrongfully convicted of three murders at a bar in 1966 and spent 19 years in prison before a court freed him. Carter became an international symbol of racial injustice.

21st DECEMBER 1991

Khaosai Galaxy retired as an unbeaten world champion after unanimously outpointing Armando Castro in a 19th defence of his WBA super-flyweight title. The star of Thai boxing finished his

48-fight career without ever being knocked out with just one points loss early on in his record. Castro was one of only three challengers to last the distance with Galaxy during his reign as champion. Galaxy's twin brother Khaokor also won the WBA bantamweight title in 1988, making them the first twins to hold world titles.

22nd DECEMBER 1989

Michael Moorer, just 22, looked impressive as he notched up his 18th successive KO by halting Mike Sedillo in six rounds to retain his WBO light-heavyweight title. The systematic destruction, finished off with several clubbing blows to the head, completed a busy year for the American, who had won the belt only a year previously and this was his sixth defence in 12 months. Moorer would win the world heavyweight title in 1994 and 1996 in two brief reigns.

23rd DECEMBER 1902

Harry Forbes was declared winner an hour after Frankie Neil was carried out of the ring after claiming he had been hit by a low blow in the seventh round in Oakland. Referee Ed Smith dismissed Neil's claims he had been hit low after a medical inspection. Neil, who was knocked down nine times in the world bantamweight title bout, had been due to face Forbes's younger brother Clarence, who fell ill so Harry stepped in. But Neil got revenge on his fellow Irish-American the following year with a second round KO for the world bantamweight title. Also on this day in 1903, Sam Langford – the Canadian who was denied many title opportunities because of the colour of his skin – fought a 12-round draw with Jack Blackburn, later the trainer of Joe Louis, in Boston. Two weeks earlier, Langford had beaten Joe Gans over 15 rounds.

24th DECEMBER 1934

World champions Freddie Miller and Panama Al Brown were booed by the crowd in Paris during their ten round bout and by the time it had ended most of the crowd had walked out of the Palais Des Sports in disgust. Brown, the first Hispanic world champion after claiming the bantamweight belt in 1929, held on to Miller whenever he could despite two warnings from the referee. NBA featherweight champion Miller took the decision, but neither of their world titles were on the line. Despite his unpopularity on this night, Brown continued to box in Europe for another three years before returning across the Atlantic.

25th DECEMBER 1923

Harry Greb and Tommy Loughran exchanged punches instead of presents in one of their six ring meetings. But Loughran weighed in eight pounds over the limit, meaning this was a non-title ten-round bout instead of it being for Greb's world middleweight title. Greb, who had extended Gene Tunney the 15 rounds distance just two weeks earlier, laboured to a points win at Pittsburgh Motor Square Garden. This was one of six meetings between the pair, with two no decisions, one draw, two wins for Greb and one win for Loughran.

25th DECEMBER 1933

Kid Chocolate was in decline and Frankie Klick gratefully capitalised on the chance to win the world super-featherweight title in Philadelphia. Klick – beaten in his three previous fights – stopped the Cuban in the seventh round but this was a gift-wrapped fight for him. Kid was finished as an elite fighter, his lifestyle catching up with him, and a month previously had been KO'd in two rounds by Tony Canzoneri. In the seventh, Kid was left face first on the canvas from a right to the jaw.

26th DECEMBER 1908

Jack Johnson became boxing's first black world heavyweight champion when he toyed with and then swatted the smaller Tommy Burns like an insect in the Sydney afternoon heat on Boxing Day. After Burns failed to remotely trouble a smiling and laughing Johnson, the challenger finished a commanding performance with a 14th round stoppage that began a seven-year reign. In the sixth round, 30-year-old Johnson felt so at ease he turned his head to talk to ringside reporters; four rounds later, he held Burns motionless for a photograph. Burns, at 5ft 7in and weighing 24 pounds less than his American rival, was the shortest ever world heavyweight champion and at times Johnson was propping him up rather than beating him down. The white establishment did not want a black world heavyweight champion and Johnson feared conspiracy, so

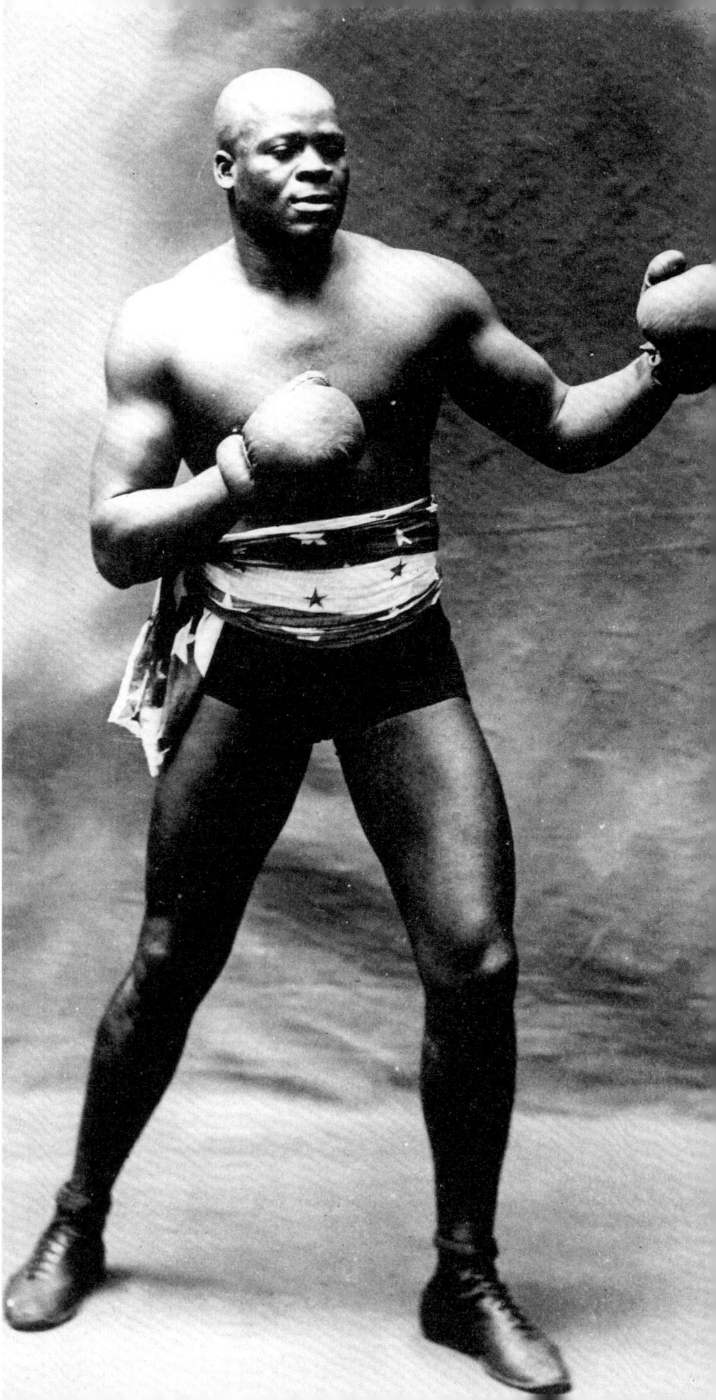

JACK JOHNSON, WORLD HEAVYWEIGHT CHAMPION FROM 1908-1915

he cautiously declined from throwing any body shots to avoid being disqualified for low blows. It did not impede Johnson, from Galveston in Texas, too much and in the 14th round the Sydney Police stormed into the ring to stop the one-sided fight after Burns had been smashed to the canvas and was on the brink of defeat.

27th DECEMBER 1997

Unknown South African Zolani Petelo upset the locals by stopping Ratanapol Sor Vorapin in the fourth round and ending the Thai boxer's remarkable run of 21 victories in consecutive IBF mini-flyweight (minimum-weight) title fights. It was the first time Vorapin had been beaten as champion and he failed in two subsequent bids to win back the belt.

28th DECEMBER 2004

Mexican Israel Vazquez made a successful first defence of his IBF world super-bantamweight title by flooring the undefeated Artyom Simonyan twice in the third and once in the fifth round before the fight was stopped. Vazquez was on his way to big fights against Rafael Marquez, Oscar Larios, Ivan Hernandez and Jhonny Gonzalez.

29th DECEMBER 2007

Marco Huck went looking for the knockout late on against American Steve Cunningham, only to be stopped himself with a minute to go of their IBF world cruiserweight title fight. Cunningham wobbled crowd-pleaser Huck with a right uppercut before the German's corner threw in the towel as the champion looked for the stoppage in the 12th round. Cunningham was leading on two of the three judges' scorecards in Germany.

30th DECEMBER 1966

Walter McGowan was on the verge of a successful first defence of his WBC world flyweight title in Bangkok after he had twice deposited Chartchai Chionoi on the canvas with left hooks in the second round. But the Thai boxer recovered and returned fire to give the Scot a bad nosebleed which became so severe that it prompted the referee to stop the fight in the ninth round. "The referee did the right thing," said McGowan's manager and dad Thomas, who had boxed himself under the name of Joe Gans. "I would never have let it go another round myself. Walter was winning, but I would have stopped it." The pair fought again in London a year later when McGowan was again stopped on cuts, this time around both eyes and on his forehead.

31st DECEMBER 1952

Former world middleweight champion Jake LaMotta, renowned for his love of the good life and punch-lines, was left to drown his sorrows rather than toast the New Year after a miserable performance. LaMotta – known as the Bronx Bull – was dumped on the canvas for the first time in 103 fights by a right hand from Danny Nardico. LaMotta was taking a pasting and his corner pulled him out at the end of the seventh round. It was the beginning of the end for LaMotta, who the previous year had been world champion but would have just three more fights after this loss. "In my whole career I never really got hurt," said LaMotta. "The only ones that really hurt me were my wives. My third wife divorced me because I said to her 'your stockings are wrinkled'. How the hell did I know she wasn't wearing any?"